Narcissistic Abuse Recovery in Toxic Relationship

Healing Love & Recovering from Covert Narcissism, Manipulation & Trauma – Dealing with Abusive Narcissist Partner, Family, Parent, Mother or Father

Naila Farrah

an illegal act regardless of the end form the information ultimately takes. This includes copied versions of the work both physical, digital and audio unless express consent of the Publisher is provided beforehand. Any additional rights reserved.

Furthermore, the information that can be found within the pages described forthwith shall be considered both accurate and truthful when it comes to the recounting of facts. As such, any use, correct or incorrect, of the provided information will render the Publisher free of responsibility as to the actions taken outside of their direct purview. Regardless, there are zero scenarios where the original author or the Publisher can be deemed liable in any fashion for any damages or hardships that may result from any of the information discussed herein.

Additionally, the information in the following pages is intended only for informational purposes and should thus be thought of as universal. As befitting its nature, it is presented without assurance regarding its prolonged validity or interim quality. Trademarks that are mentioned are done without written consent and can in no way be considered an endorsement from the trademark holder.

Table of Contents

Your Free Resource Is Awaiting

To better help you, I've created a simple mind map you can use _right away_ to easily understand, quickly recall and readily use what you'll be learning in this book.

Click Here To Get Your Free Resource

Alternatively, here's the link:

https://viebooks.club/freeresourcemindmapfornarcissisticabuserecoveryintoxicrelationship

Introduction

Congratulations on purchasing this book and thank you for doing so.

It is my belief that every woman, man, and child should be able to feel worthy and empowered. My story begins the day I found out that I had allowed myself to become programmed from the abuse that has been passed down through the generations in my family. I had to learn how to self-heal from narcissistic abuse, but where did all this start? Unfortunately, that's a question that may never have an answer.

Abuse is typically trans-generational. It becomes seen as something acceptable and normal. Parents model this behavior, and it tells their children that is what love looks like. These children then grow up to accept abuse from others, or they end up becoming the abusers. Not all abuse victims end up abusing others, but unfortunately, a good number of them do. Eventually, the abuse turns into a pandemic.

Abuse can happen to anyone. Women, children, men, anyone. It is not restricted by gender, age, race, sexuality, religion, etc., although it is more prominent in some groups, namely priorities, than it is in others. It is a form of oppression, a way for the abuser to assert control over the abused. And no one deserves such torture.

Not only did I spend the first 18 years of my life living with narcissistic abuse from my father, but I continued to suffer from it for several years after. After a trip abroad for work, I realized something in my home life was off. While I was away from my family for a month, I felt different. I was happier. I did more things I enjoyed. I looked forward to each day.

Once I returned to the States, I shared my experience with my older sister. She looked at me and told me why I had felt that way. "Dad wasn't there." See, she had noticed his abuse early on. I'm not sure how, but she had gotten out of his grasp earlier than I did. From that point on, I started working on removing his abuse from my life so that every day could feel like I was away on a business trip.

This abuse doesn't make sense to those of us with empathy. Empathy is something that so many people lack. This can be better, and I believe many people feel this way as well. The world can be better. It is our responsibility to make the world a better place so that future generations don't have to face this abuse.

Things begin to change when people stand up and decide they aren't going to let the cycle continue. Don't get me wrong, this isn't easy, but you will notice something amazing when you do this. As others begin to make this change and more people start to speak up about their communities, families, and relationships, more people will feel that they can do the same.

As we all vow to stop condoning this behavior, the world will change. This ostracizes the abusers and quits celebrating them. By taking responsibility for yourself, you will heal the world. As you work to make yourself healthy again, you will be able to stand with confidence and integrity with who you are and prevent yourself from ever being abused again.

As the abuse starts to go away, you will be able to live your purpose. You will find a sense of meaning. Your soul will feel happy and free, which will create a ripple effect throughout the world.

Part One: The Narcissist

Chapter 1: What is Narcissism

Oftentimes, the term narcissism gets used to describe somebody who has an inflated sense of self-worth. However, it is a little more complicated than that. A person who exhibits these narcissistic traits could suffer from a personality disorder called Narcissistic Personality Disorder. When a person suffers from a personality disorder, it affects how they relate to others, think, and behave.

Narcissism is also known as the pursuit of gratification from egotistic or vanity admiration of their own idealized self-image. Narcissism comes from the Greek mythological figure, Narcissus. He was the son of a god and fell in love with his reflection in the spring water.

As a psychoanalytic theory, narcissism was first introduced by Sigmund Freud in his essay *On Narcissism* in 1914. Narcissistic Personality Disorder has been listed in the American Psychiatric Association's *Diagnostic and Statistical Manual of Mental Disorders* since 1968. [1]

This means that if narcissism causes a person distress and dysfunction, it is considered a personality disorder. A person with Narcissistic Personality Disorder will often show some of the following traits in such a fashion that makes it seem that they view themselves as superior:

- They have to be admired

- They have an oversized sense of their own successes

- They can't handle criticism

- They think they are very important

The *Journal of Clinical Psychiatry* published a 2008 study that found that 6.2% of people likely had NPD. This is a more common disorder for men at 7.7% than for women at 4.8%. The study also discovered that is was more common in younger people, as well as in those who have never been married or have been divorced, separated, or widowed. [2]

Narcissistic Personality Disorder

Through the years, the views of narcissism have changed slightly, and eventually, Narcissistic Personality Disorder came to be. This personality disorder is described as having long-term patterns of abnormal behavior that are often characterized by a lack of empathy, excessive need for admiration, and exaggerated self-importance. People who are affected by this problem spend most of their time thinking about reaching power or success. They take advantage of those around them. This type of behavior will normally start in early adulthood and can occur across many different social situations.

The exact cause of this disorder is still unknown. It is classified within cluster B of the DSM. Cluster B personality disorders are disorders that are characterized by unpredictable, overly emotional or dramatic behavior or thinking.

There hasn't been a lot of research into the neurological reasons for NPD. However, there has been recent research that has found structural abnormalities within the brain of those with NPD. They found that there is less gray matter in the left anterior insula. A different study has found that people with NPD had less gray matter in their prefrontal cortex. [2]

These different brain regions are associated with cognitive functioning, emotional regulation, compassion, and empathy. This suggests that NPD could be due to a compromised capacity for emotional regulation and empathy.

Chapter 2: The Growth of a Narcissist

NPD is extremely resistant to treatment and causes the individual to create chaos in their life as they harm those around them. Before we start talking about how the support of the ego and desires can get messed up, let's take a look at what is important for normal child development.

It is normal for small children to act selfishly. This is a normal part of their development in which they are making sure that their needs get met and they haven't learned how to understand the desires and needs of others. Once they become teenagers, kids are normally still more self-centered as they try to find their independence.

As opposed to this self-centeredness that should slowly disappear, children must create healthy and lasting self-esteem levels in order to care for and protect themselves while also caring about those around them, resist negative influences, and remain connected with their society and family. Healthy self-esteem levels show that a child believes that they are a worthy and loved person in society and in their family. This makes them more resilient to mistreatment. Self-esteem and self-centeredness are not the same thing because self-esteem does not lead to putting yourself first at the detriment of other people's rights and needs.

The normal self-centeredness of childhood has to change in order to create a way for mental health in adulthood. Kids need to learn how to gain the ability to see other's viewpoints and empathize with other's suffering in order to function well as an adult in society and families. So, a healthy child should slowly start to show sincere forms of caring about the wellbeing of those around them. Not learning how to empathize while growing up is a sign of major personality disorders as an adult, which include NPD.

Narcissists, in general, make others feel miserable and get aggressive with those who don't give in to them. These are traits that are commonly found in dictators. Like the majority of personality disorders, narcissism is hard to treat because those that are affected don't understand that something is wrong and thus lack the motivation to change.

The overall cause of Narcissistic Personality Disorder is still unknown. Experts will often apply a biopsychosocial model of causation. This means that they combine neurobiological, genetic, social, and environmental factors that could play a role in creating this narcissistic personality.

There is some evidence that suggests that Narcissistic Personality Disorders are inherited, and people are more likely to end up with NPD if there is a family history. There have been studies performed on the occurrence of personality disorders in twins that found there is a moderate to high chance of NPD being heritable.

However, the genes and gene interactions that cause these issues and how they play a part in influencing the developmental and physiological processes that are under NPD haven't been determined.

It is also believed that social and environmental factors could influence the onset of NPD. In some cases, pathological narcissism can develop from a flawed attachment to their parents or primary caregiver. This can end up messing up their perception of themselves as unconnected and unimportant to others. The child will end up believing that they have some sort of defect that makes them unwanted and unvalued. Over-controlling, insensitive parenting, as well as permissive, over-indulgent parenting can be contributing factors.

Arnold Cooper and Leonard Groopman identified the following factors that could cause the development of NPD:

- Used by their parents as a means to regulate their parent's self-esteem.

- Learned manipulative behaviors from their peers or parents.

- Unreliable or unpredictable caregiving from parents.

- Being praised for perceived exceptional abilities or looks by adults.

- Overvaluation and overindulgence by peers, family members, or parents.

- Excessive criticism of bad behaviors or excessive praise for good behaviors in childhood.

- Excessive admiration that isn't based on realistic feedback.

- Having an oversensitive temperament since birth.

It is also believed that cultural elements could influence NPD and that NPD traits are more common within modern societies, as opposed to traditional ones.

True Self vs. False Self

A narcissist lives in their own little world where they have created a false self, but why have they created this false self instead of living their true self?

Once a narcissist has formed their false self and is fully functioning, this false self stifles the true self's growth. This makes the true self virtually non-existent and without a role in the life of the narcissist. Once the false self takes over, it's hard to resuscitate the true self.

This idealized or false self sets the narcissist some impossible goals. This ends up making the narcissist frustrated and grows self-hate, which only grows when they face failure or setback. They don't actually experience a conflict between their true and false self.

The true self is extremely weak and cannot battle the overbearing false self. The false self has the ability to adapt to everything. It works by helping the true self cope with the world. If the false self didn't exist, the true self would have to face more hurt. This often happens to narcissists who have gone through a life crisis, causing their false self to become dysfunctional, and they live through feelings of annulment.

There are several functions for this false self, but the two most important are:

1. It works as a decoy. The false self attracts the fire. It's the true self's proxy. It's tough and can absorb pain, negative emotions, and hurt. With the invention of the false

self, it gives the person immunity to the exploitation, smothering, sadism, manipulation, or indifference, basically, to the abuse that has been inflicted on them by their guardian. It works as a cloak, protecting them and leaving them omnipotent and invisible.

2. The narcissist misrepresents the false self as the true self. Basically, the narcissist tells the outside world: "I'm not who you believe me to be. I am somebody else. I am this (false) person. Therefore, I should receive more considerate and painless treatment." This makes the false self a contraption to alter others' behavior toward them.

This is important for their survival and to the psychological functioning of the narcissist. They love the false self a lot more than they want their dilapidated true self. These two selves don't work together. The healthy person does have a false self that differs in that it is closer or more realistic to the true self. Even healthy people sometimes wear a mask to the outside world, but they consciously present this mask. The false self is a sub-conscious presentation that depends on outside feedback.

It is common knowledge that the narcissist has a prominent false self and a dilapidated true self, but how intertwined are they? Do these two interact? Does one influence the other? Which behaviors can be attributed to each of these selves? Does the false self take on attributes of the true self in order to trick those around them?

There are some cases where a person exhibits traits of a person with NPD, but they wouldn't be psychologically classified as such. In these cases, the true self may make an appearance. In a full-blown narcissist, the false self imitates the true self. It does this in two ways:

- Re-interpretation: It makes the narcissist reevaluate different reactions and emotions in a socially-acceptable light. This means that it is opposite day for the narcissist every day. They will see negative emotions as a positive and vice versa. That's what makes it so hard to understand the narcissist because they interpret emotions and the like in different ways than most.

- Emulation: The narcissist has an uncanny ability to control people's minds. This is an abused talent and the narcissist has complete control over the sadism. They use it to get rid of the natural defenses of their victims by pretending to be empathetic. This is coupled with their ability to imitate emotions and their effects. They keep records of every action and reaction of others regarding their emotional makeup. From this information, they then pretend to share this emotion. This is a very powerful deceptive tool.

Their Perfect Victim

It is a common misconception that narcissists will go after the weak because they can more easily be manipulated. In fact, narcissists like to break a person who is strong-willed and who possesses characteristics or talents they admire. This makes them feel good about themselves. They turn a person's strength into nothing. The goal of the narcissist is to make sure they feel good, so they are going to be attracted to those who can make this happen.

While the following is by no means the only types of people narcissists go after, there are four main types of people narcissists are often attracted to:

1. Someone who is able to validate their feelings, overlook their flaws, and who is less likely to leave once the abuse starts.

2. Anyone who will make them look better in the eyes of others.

3. Somebody who will make them feel good about themselves through gestures or compliments.

4. People who are in some way impressive, either in their family, friend circles, talents, hobbies, or career.

More times than not, narcissists are looking for a unicorn that doesn't exist. They already have unrealistic expectations for their significant other and very little consistency. This causes them to remain unhappy in their relationships once that first spark has disappeared.

It looks as if narcissists will go after certain types of people and then work to destroy them due to their own low self-esteem. All narcissists enjoy destroying other people, but not all of them do this because of their own low self-esteem even though the majority does so. The toxic and exhibitionist narcissist may destroy people simply for the joy of it and not due to low self-esteem.

As long as the narcissist feels like they are in control of the relationship, they view it as successful.

Traits of a Narcissist

Four types of narcissism as a personality disorder have been described: entitlement/exploitativeness, self-admiration/absorption, superiority/arrogance, and leadership/authority.

Many therapists have criticized these criteria because they presume knowledge of intent. Others can witness their behavior, but they can't see intention. This means classification requires some assumptions that have to be tested before they can be considered true, especially when there are several reasons why a person could be exhibiting these behaviors.

Psychiatrists James F. Masterson and Hotchkiss found what they referred to as the seven deadly sins of narcissism.

1. **Bad boundaries**: Narcissists aren't able to recognize their boundaries and that other people are separate and aren't just an extension of themselves. Other people either are there to meet the narcissist's needs or don't exist at all. Those who provide them with what they need are treated as if they belong to the narcissist and are supposed to live up to their expectations. Narcissists don't believe that there is a boundary between themselves and others.

2. **Exploitation**: This can take on several forms but will always involve exploiting others without considering their interests or feelings. The other person will always take on a subservient position where resistance is hard or completely impossible. This subservience is assumed more than real.

3. **Entitlement**: Narcissists have created very unreasonable expectations of favorable treatment and compliance because they think they are special. Failure for people to comply with this is viewed as an attack on their superiority, and the perp is viewed as a "difficult" or "awkward" person. Defying their will is an injury to a narcissist and might end up triggering narcissistic rage.

4. **Envy**: Narcissists are able to live with a sense of superiority in the face of other's achievements by using contempt to minimize their achievements.

5. **Arrogance**: Narcissists who start to feel deflated will fix this by degrading, diminishing, or debasing someone else.

6. **Magical thinking**: Narcissists are perfect in their own eyes by using the illusion and distortion known as magical thinking. They will also project in order to dump their shame onto another person.

7. **Shamelessness**: Narcissists are more often than not openly and proudly shameless. They do not allow themselves to be bound by the wishes and needs of others. Narcissists despise shame and view it as "toxic." This is because shame implies they aren't perfect and would require change. Narcissists like to guilt and shame, as guilt gives them the ability to dissociate from their actions. This means that only their actions were wrong, but they are still perfect.

These are only a few of the common traits of people with narcissistic personality disorders. To make sure you fully understand the traits of a narcissist, here are a few more traits:

- A large appetite for the attention of others.

- Extreme levels of jealousy.

- They expect special treatment.

- They exaggerate their importance, talents, and achievements.

- They are very sensitive and have a tendency to be easily hurt and feel rejected with very little provocation.

- They find it hard to maintain healthy relationships.

- They fantasize about their own appearance, power, success, and intelligence.

- They lack empathy or any ability to understand the feelings of others, and they often disregard the feelings of others.

- They believe that only certain people are able to understand their uniqueness.

- They tend to consider their self as skilled in romance.

- They seek positive reinforcement and praise from others.

- They expect others to agree with them on everything and go along with them no matter what.

- Everything that they want has to be the best.

Verbal Abuse

The verbal abuse of a narcissist is powerful. A narcissist can drain a person and spin things around on them before they know what happens. The narcissist convinces their victim that what's up is down and that everything is really their fault.

This is why verbal abuse is a narcissist's top control tactic. They can quickly intimidate the victim while also establishing dominance. This attack more often than not catches the victim off guard. The pattern will be the same no matter if the victim is the narcissist's preacher, manager, coach, employer, parent, or spouse. It starts infrequently and in secret, in a mild tone, and is sometimes accompanied with a fake apology. This grows into public humiliation, becomes more frequent, and then they blame their victim.

They use their tone and volume to establish dominance. There are two extremes to this. One is to up their volume through raging, yelling, and screaming. The other is through not responding, silence, and ignoring.

Their words often come with double meanings. They use these words to cause fear, constrain, oppress, manipulate, and intimidate. Threatening and swearing is second nature when a person won't do what the narcissist wants.

They will do as much as they can to avoid being embarrassed, including becoming defensive over small infractions. Their big self-views are so important that they will accuse their victim of causing them to appear bad. If they see an attack, they won't take responsibility and dismiss things with lies.

They are the winners of the blame game. Anything that goes awry is the fault of the other person. They say the other person is being too "sensitive."

Looking back, my father was particularly good at verbal abuse. His signature move—the one in which we know means we need to shut up and stop contradicting him—was when he stops talking entirely. Typically, he would do this when we would continue to insist that he was wrong about something or misunderstanding something, which I've learned from my older sister gets to him because he takes it to mean that we think he's stupid. When he got that silent, his jaw would also visibly clench, and we would usually just acquiesce to whatever he believed or said. Swearing when we don't do what he wants is another one of his favorites (and one of the many reasons I still can't stand loud noises). Many times, he would insist that we never had these arguments or that he actually said what I had said, making me question my memory and sanity in a method of abuse called gaslighting.

Gaslighting

Gaslighting is another common trait of narcissists. Gaslighting is a type of persistent brainwashing and manipulation that makes a person doubts themselves. This will eventually lead to them losing their own sense of self-worth, identity, and perception. The gaslighter will often make accusations and statements that tend to be based on calculated marginalization and deliberate falsehoods. The term gaslighting came about from the 1944 film *Gaslight*, where the husband tried to trick his wife into believing that she was insane by causing her to start questioning her reality.

Gaslighting makes you think that you are the crazy one. Gaslighting is their way of hiding abuse. Gaslighting is lying about things with a goal in mind. They do this in order to make sure you don't trust your own perceptions of your reality. This gives them more time to take over as the authority of your life.

Gaslighting can happen within romantic relationships, family, friendships, or any other relationships where there is one-on-one interaction. Gaslighting is very prevalent in politicians, cult leaders, advertising commercials, corporate shills, and so on.

There is a really scary fact about gaslighting that is talked about in the book *The Sociopath Next Door* by Dr. Martha Stout. She talked to several incarcerated sociopaths and asked if they knew the term gaslighting. The majority of them did not recognize the term and once she explained what it was, they said they love to do it.

This is what my dad met me with when I confronted him about the abuse over three years ago. He flaunted his joy for gaslighting in front of my mom and me. Gaslighting is often used by narcissism to evade responsibility. This will also help them to come up with conversations that never even happened.

When you are gaslighted, you will most often feel:

- Vulnerable

- As if you're losing your mind

- Terror

- Fear

- Paranoia

- Disorientation

- Self-doubt

- Brain fog

- Confusion

- Sense of false guilt

- Misunderstood

- Lonely

Gaslighting can become so bad that it could push you to the point of a nervous breakdown. Gaslighting can be as innocent as "No, silly, I said Saturday. I'm busy on Friday."

It can also be as bad as "I don't understand why you are crying so much, you never liked that dog. You're just acting and forcing out those tears to get attention. You should feel ashamed of yourself when I'm the one that's actually sad."

This person completely invalidated the feelings of the upset person. This is likely not the only time they have done so. Things like this compound and create more problems for the victim.

Stonewalling

Have you ever experienced this, you're trying to have an important conversation with a family member, friend, or partner and they simply ignored you? Has a toxic person ever silenced you with the silent treatment? This is what is known as stonewalling.

Dr. John Gottman, a researcher, said in his *The Four Horsemen of the Apocalypse,* "four me's of the apocalypse" or four communication styles in relationships that can be used to predict the end of the relationship. These include stonewalling, defensiveness, contempt, and criticism.

Stonewalling occurs when a person pulls out of a conversation and won't address any of your questions. They may outright ignore your requests, evade response altogether, invalidate your replies, or respond dismissively. They will often give vague responses that dance around your original questions.

Most of the time when stonewalling occurs, the conversation will stop before it ever starts. This type of tactic will cause further conflict, depression, and anxiety. While this is often used by the narcissist to avoid conflict, all it is doing is compounding the problem.

Here's an example:

Elizabeth is worried about how her partner, Phil, has been treating her as of late. He constantly criticizes her and is neglecting her needs. She tries to bring up these concerns with him during dinner, but all she gets is stony silence. He then gaslights her and says she is overreacting. When she tries to explain herself, he jumps up abruptly and shouts, "I'm done!"

He leaves the table and walks outs of the apartment without saying anything else. He also won't take her phone calls. They haven't even had the chance to talk before the discussion ends. He calls her the following day and acts as though nothing happened. When Elizabeth tries to bring it up, he says, "You need to talk to a therapist," and then hangs up before she can respond.

Phil stonewalls her twice and emotionally invalidates her and redirects the conversation. He won't address the problems even though he is only causing more. This causes Elizabeth to feel stressed.

Typically, the silent treatment and stonewalling go hand-in-hand. Once the victim is stonewalled, the other person won't talk to them, but the silent treatment can occur without stonewalling.

A narcissist uses stonewalling and the silent treatment as manipulation tactics. These are usually regular parts of the cycle, but each narcissist works differently. A cycle may look something like this:

The narcissist starts out showing their victim a whole lot of love, giving them more attention to help win them over. Then they hit the devaluation phase. The tables turn, and the victim is provoked into trying to make the narcissist happy. The toxic partner will abruptly pull themselves away from their victim, unwilling to say something for a while with no explanation. This silence causes their partner to feel fear, anxiety, and constantly doubt themselves. The narcissist thrives off of this control and power they feel as they work their victim like a puppet.

Projection

Projection is another defense mechanism of the narcissist, but it is one that can tell you all their secrets. The narcissist projects all their problems and feelings about their self onto their victim.

They accuse you of being the one that is doing what they are. They throw any uncomfortable feelings they are experiencing onto you because they can't deal with them. They project their shame onto you. They try to make you feel guilty for what they do and who they are because they can't experience guilt.

Anybody can project things onto others without realizing it. When it comes to narcissists, they project because they can't see things inside themselves, so they have to project them.

Projection is a combination of blame-shifting and misdirection. They are working to distract and divert you from what is actually happening, and they are trying to make you take responsibility for it. At face value, that is what they think is going on, but if you really read them, you will start to realize how valuable this projection is and how much they are revealing about who they are.

Here's an example:

Margaret is putting dinner on the table when her husband, Fred, comes in. He slams the door and stomps over to his wife. "What have you been doing today?" he shouts. Margaret is confused by this outburst. She hasn't been anywhere. She stays home and takes care of their baby, and that's what she tells him.

This isn't good enough for Fred. "You're cheating on me!" he shouts. "I know you are. I want to know everything you did today, and you better be able to prove it." Margaret is left flabbergasted by this outburst. She does her best to prove to Fred she isn't cheating on him and that she was at home all day, but she can tell he doesn't fully believe her.

If Margaret were able to take a moment to remove herself from this conversation, she could see that Fred is projecting. There is a good chance that Fred is either cheating on her or thinking about it.

Projecting can also be as simple as a narcissist saying, "Where's our dumpling of a waitress?" The narcissist is likely on the heavyset side.

They are externalizing their own shortcomings because they can't face them head-on.

Triangulation

Triangulation is the last narcissistic trait we are going to look at and ranks right up there with gaslighting as one of the narcissist's favorite tactics. Triangulation is a form of manipulation in which they use a third party to help them, often without the knowledge of the third party. Their goal is to inflict some type of mental and emotional abuse on their victim. This is a common tactic used by narcissists, borderlines, psychopaths, and sociopaths.

The narcissist, when using triangulation, will use the help of a third party to dismantle or discredit their victim. They will often do this by playing the victim themselves and try to get the third party to appear supportive of their innocence.

There are three roles in triangulation manipulation.

The oppressor is often played by the narcissist. They believe that they are the victim. This is the role they take because they project their negative parts onto their victim. They will then start to believe that the victim is acting out in a way that is unacceptable. This is a result of their projections.

One of the simplest forms of triangulation that narcissists will use starts with the narcissist taking up their role in the plot. Perhaps they act out selfishly towards their partner and then their partner ends up becoming upset because of this behavior. Since the narcissist believes that they are right, they start labeling their partner as the bad guy. They then find a negative cause in all their behavior that contradicts how the narcissist views themselves.

The next role is the champion. This role isn't always played by a person. It can be an individual or a statement that the oppressor will use to boost their "defense." Sometimes the narcissist will try to find another person they can trick into believing their value and worth. This person will most likely believe that the narcissist is validated.

When a real person plays the role of the champion, they aren't aware of the true nature of the narcissist. They have been shielded from their characteristics in order to be able to take on the role of champion. Typically, the narcissist has shown the champion qualities that have made them seek out the narcissist's approval.

Sometimes the narcissist will use a statement as their champion. This statement can be fictitious or real. This statement helps to reinforce negative behavior. Their statement could claim that others are siding with the narcissist. For example, they could claim that their friend has agreed that the victim isn't being nice or is damaging their relationship to make the victim feel like they are doing something wrong.

The third role is the persecuted. This is played by the victim or the person who has tried to illuminate the narcissistic behavior they have witnessed. Their reactions to this behavior are often what causes the narcissist to engage in triangulation. The persecuted is the actual victim in this strategy that was created to discredit them and make them appear to be the problem.

Here's an example:

Bob and Freda have been together for ten years. They are out having drinks with a friend to celebrate their anniversary. Freda and Bob have never given each other a gift on their anniversary. It was an unspoken rule between them. Today, Bob has a bracelet for Freda and catches her off guard. She loves the bracelet hugs and kisses Bob for the surprise gift then an awkward silence falls over their group. Bob stares at Freda, waiting. He taps the table a few times and sighs.

"You forgot, didn't you?" Bob snaps.

Freda stares at Bob, confused. "Forgot what?"

"I can't believe this. You were with me when I bought that. You know how expensive it was," Bob stated to his friend. The friend nods in agreement.

"I'm sorry, Bob, but we have never gotten each other anything for our anniversary. We always just go out with a friend or two."

"You are embarrassing me in front of my friend. He can't believe how you treat me."

This conversation could go on for hours for Bob and Freda, but in the end, Freda will be left feeling confused and ashamed. Bob uses his friend as his champion to help come off like he is the victim.

This form of manipulation often happens within an intimate relationship, but a narcissist can use triangulation in any type of relationship.

Chapter 3: Narcissistic Abuse

Stephen Johnson, a psychologist, believes that a narcissist is a person who has buried their true self-expression due to early life injuries and exchanged it with a highly developed false self.

Narcissism is often viewed in pop-culture as a person who is in love with themselves, but it's more accurate to say that a pathological narcissist is in love with an idealized version of themselves, which is projected on others to avoid feeling their real self.

Are You in a Relationship with a Narcissist?

Being in a relationship with a narcissist is hard. What's more, it's hard to discover that you are even in a relationship with a narcissist. The narcissist works hard to make sure their victim is none the wiser. The following are telltale signs that you are in a relationship with a narcissist. These signs are true for any type of relationship, not just a romantic one. While many of us are likely guilty of some of these behaviors at some point in our life, a pathological narcissist dwells habitually within many of these different traits, while remaining unaware or unconcerned with how they are affecting others.

1. Conversation Hoarder: Narcissists love to talk about their self, and they won't give you a chance to have a two-way conversation. You struggle to get them to listen to your feelings and views. When you do get to say something, if it's not agreeing with them, they will ignore, dismiss, or correct your comment. Some of my dad's favorite things to respond with were "there's more than that...," "but...," and "actually..."

2. Conversation Interrupter: While a lot of people have bad communication habits like interrupting people, the narcissist will interrupt and turn the focus of the conversation to them.

3. Rule Breaker: Narcissists like to get away with things that go against the social norms and rules, like cutting, under-tipping, taking things from work, not following traffic laws, and breaking appointments.

4. Boundary Violator: They show a disregard for other's physical space, possessions, feelings, and thoughts. They will overstep their bounds and use others without thinking about them. They borrow things without returning them. They break obligations and promises.

5. False Image Projection: Narcissists do things to impress others, so they do things to make them look good on the outside. This sort of "trophy" complex can show up in cultural, academic, professional, material, financial, religious, social, sexual, romantic, and physical settings. These are like "merit badges" for the narcissist.

6. Entitlement: They expect to get preferential treatment from everybody. They want to instantly be catered to without providing anything in return.

7. Charmer: They are very persuasive and charismatic. When they are interested in somebody, they will do things to make that person feel wanted and special. When they

lose interest, they can drop a person without a second thought. They are very social creatures.

8. Grandiose Personality: They view their self as a hero or a princess. They have a high amount of self-importance, believing that other people can't survive without them.

9. Negative Emotions: They love to arouse negative emotions in others because it makes them feel powerful. Any perceived slight to their authority will upset them. They like to throw tantrums if they feel you aren't doing what they want or if you disagree with them. They hate criticism, but they are also quick to blame, ridicule, criticize, and judge others.

10. Manipulation: They make other people's decisions. They use their victims as a way to make sure their needs are met. They also love to guilt trip others into doing things. They love to say things like, "I've helped you so much, but you're ungrateful."

It's hard to believe when you discover you have been in a relationship with a narcissist. Luckily, there are plenty of ways to help you get out of the relationship and heal, many of which we will talk about.

Symptoms of Narcissistic Abuse

Picture this: your whole reality has become distorted and warped. You have suffered through gaslighting, have been demeaned, ridiculed, lied to, manipulated, and violated into believing that you're seeing things wrong. The person you believed you understood and the life that you have created together has been destroyed.

You no longer have a sense of self. You were worshiped, devalued, then kicked off of your pedestal that they put you on. You may have been discarded and replaced several times, just to be sucked back into the cycle which has become more torturous. You may have been relentlessly bullied, harassed, and stalked to stay.

This isn't a normal relationship or breakup. This was all a setup and silently worked to kill your psyche. While you may not have visible scars, you have a bunch of broken pieces, internal scars, and fractured memories.

This is narcissistic abuse.

Malignant narcissists who are psychologically violent can include triangulation, smear campaigns, sabotage, stonewalling, toxic projection, emotional and verbal abuse, as well as a bunch of other control and coercion tactics. This is all performed by a person who doesn't feel empathy, feels they are entitled, and exploits others to meet their needs.

This abuse can cause a victim to suffer from symptoms of complex PTSD or PTSD, especially if they suffered at the hands of narcissistic parents. PTSD and C-PTSD differ only in the fact that the cause of C-PTSD is reoccurring, such as childhood abuse, whereas PTSD is typically a single traumatic event.

The effect of this abuse can cause overwhelming feelings of worthlessness and helplessness, emotional flashback, sense of toxic shame, hypervigilance, anxiety, and depression.

When you are still living within the cycle of abuse, it can be hard to notice exactly what is going on because the abuser is great at twisting your reality around to suit theirs. We are going to go over several symptoms that you could experience when you have suffered from narcissistic abuse.

1. You start to feel dissociated in order to help you survive.

You may notice that you feel physically and emotionally detached from your surroundings, experience memory problems, disruptions of perceptions, sense of self, and consciousness. Dissociation can cause emotional numbing when faced with horrific circumstances. Repression, addictions, obsessions, and activities that numb the mind can become the norm because they provide you with a means of escape. Your brain works to find ways to block emotions so that you don't have to face the pain of the situation.

2. You find yourself walking on eggshells.

One of the most common symptoms of trauma is trying to avoid anything that could relive the trauma. This could be activities, places, or people that pose a threat. You find that you are hyper-aware of the things that you say or do around your abuser to make sure that you don't face their abuse or become the object envy or punishment.

However, you soon realize that this isn't going to work, and you still end up getting attacked by the abuser and whenever they want, you become their emotional test dummy. You feel more anxious about provoking them, and this causes you to avoid setting boundaries and confrontation. You might even start people-pleasing.

3. You push aside your own desires and needs, sacrificing yourself and possibly your bodily safety in order to make your abuser happy.

At one point in your life, you were likely dream-oriented, driven by goals, and full of life. Now all you feel is that you live only to obtain the needs of others. At one point, the narcissist seemed to care about you, but now your life is caring for them.

You could also have pushed all your friendships, hobbies, and goals back to make sure that you can "satisfy" your abuser. Eventually, you realize that they won't ever be satisfied no matter what happens.

4. You find it hard to trust others.

You now view everybody as a perceived threat and you now find yourself more anxious about having to interact with others, especially after living through the evil actions of a person that you use to trust. Regular caution has turned into hypervigilance. Since your abuser has gaslighted you to the point of believing that what you have experienced is invalid, you find it very hard to trust anybody, and this includes yourself.

5. You have thoughts about suicide or harming yourself.

With the anxiety and depression, you now suffer from come an increase feeling of hopelessness. You find life unbearable, like there is no way to get out, even if that's what you wanted. You've developed a sense of helplessness that causes you to feel like you don't want to live another day. You could even self-harm to help you cope. (If you are at all struggling with these kinds of thoughts, please refer to the Helpful Resources pages for information on the Suicide Hotline.)

6. You isolate yourself.

There are a lot of abusers who will try to isolate their victims from family and friends, but victims of narcissistic abuse will often isolate themselves because the abuse makes them feel shameful. Given the misconceptions and victim-blaming about the psychological and emotional violence in society, the abused will often become retraumatized by friends, family members, police and law enforcement, and the narcissist's harem members who work to invalidate their views of this abuse.

Victims are afraid that nobody will believe or understand what they are going through, so instead of trying to get help, they choose to hide away from others so that they aren't retaliated against and judged from their abuser. Victim-shaming is an unfortunate part of society, which is all the sadder for people who need to get out of scary situations.

7. You are self-destructive and self-sabotaging.

Victims will often get lost in their own minds, thinking about what has happened to them and hearing the abuser constantly in their mind. This only increases their negative self-talk and the odds that they will self-sabotage. Narcissists work by conditioning their victims to destroy their self. This can even go so far as suicide.

Because of their over and cover put-downs, hypercriticism, and verbal abuse, victims will often end up punishing themselves because they are full of toxic shame. Victims will often sabotage their own goals, academic pursuits, and dreams. Their abuser has taught them that they are worthless, and they start to believe that the good things shouldn't come to them.

8. You are afraid of reaching success and doing things that bring you joy.

Since the majority of pathological predators envy their victims, they inflict some form of punishment when they are successful. This makes their victims associate talents, interests, joys, and success with abuse. This makes their victims fear success unless they want to be punished. Because of this, the victim will end up becoming anxious and depressed, lack confidence, and will likely hide away from being recognized for their talents and let their abusers "steal" the show. It's important to know that your abuser isn't undercutting your gifts; they really do believe that you are inferior. This is due to those gifts threatening their control.

9. You find yourself protecting the abuser and gaslighting yourself.

Denying, minimizing, and rationalizing the abuse are survival tactics for victims. To try and reduce some of the symptoms that can occur when a person who you thought loved you hurts you, victims will try to talk themselves into believing that the abuser isn't "all that bad" or they were the cause of the problem and did something to "provoke" them.

This problem can be reduced by studying about narcissistic personalities. This will give you the change to reconcile with what your reality really is with the false self of the narcissist. You will be able to recognize the abuse and not the nice façade.

This intense trauma bond is formed between the two because one has been trained to "need" their abuser in order to survive. Victims will sometimes keep abusers from facing legal consequences, put on a happy face for social media, or try to take part in the blame.

Invalidation

You can probably spot a narcissistic relationship now, and you have discovered the most common symptoms victims will experience. This is all very important in making sure that you get out of the relationship and heal, but there are some other aspects of this abuse that is important to understand. The first thing we are going to really talk about is invalidation. Narcissism and invalidation, where there is one, the other will be close behind.

Have you ever felt like you were invisible? Like you didn't matter and were worthless? If yes, then you already know the obliteration that comes from narcissistic invalidation. This is the default MO and underpins all forms of abuse. The effects of such abuse are disempowering and damaging.

Invalidation slowly erases who you are. After all, once you have been drained of your identity, full compliance to their demands is guaranteed. You have very little fight left.

Invalidation can easily be spotted like aggressive bullying tactics. It also has the ability to be insidious. Gaslighting is the main covert invalidation tactic for narcissists.

What's ironic is through their invalidation of you, they are validating themselves. The reason for all of this is because they are in denial about being perfect. We healthy people know that perfection isn't possible, but the narcissist thinks they can reach it. Thus, they invalidate others to make them feel as if they are perfect.

Neurological Impact of Narcissistic Abuse

It's common knowledge that consistent emotional abuse can leave to C-PTSD and PTSD. This is why it's important that people in this type of relationship needs to get out. Psychological and emotional distress is only part of what can happen with long-term narcissistic abuse. It can actually physically harm the brain.

Consistent emotional abuse can cause the hippocampus to shrink and the amygdala to swell. The hippocampus controls memories and learning. The amygdala is where negative emotions arise.

First, let's look at what can happen with a smaller hippocampus. The hippocampus holds our short-term memory and is the first step to learning. Without this short-term memory, you can't learn. When the volume of the hippocampus decreases, it also increases cortisol levels. This means people are more stressed.

Next is the amygdala. It controls primal functions and emotions, including breathing, heart rate, hate, fear, and lust. This is where the fight-or-flight response lives. When exposed to this abuse, it keeps their amygdala on high alert. This causes the victim to eventually fall into a permanent state of fear or anxiety.

These physical changes to the brain mean that even once the victim has left the abuse, they will live with panic attacks, increased phobias, and symptoms of PTSD.

The Cycle of Abuse

Unfortunately, abuse isn't a one-off thing. It happens in a cycle. Lenore Walker, in 1979, coined the cycle of abuse. His cycle was: tension building, acting out, reconciliation, and calm. However, a narcissist changes this abuse slightly.

The back end of the cycle is changed because the narcissist has to bring things back to them. Instead, it is often the abused who tries to appease the situation while the narcissist acts as if they are the victim. This strengthens the narcissist, further convincing them that they aren't at fault. Here are the four steps of the narcissistic abuse cycle:

1. Feels Threatened: Some sort of event took place that has caused the narcissist to feel threatened. This could be simple disrespect, neglect, jealousy of somebody else's success, embarrassment, disapproval at work, or rejection of sex. The victim knows when this happens and starts to walk on eggshells, waiting for something to happen.

2. Abuses Others: The narcissist then engages in abusive behavior. This can be emotional, spiritual, financial, sexual, verbal, mental, or physical abuse. They customize the abuse to intimidate their victim, targeting their victim's weaknesses. Eventually, the victim becomes tired of the abuse and defensively fights back.

3. Becomes the Victim: Then the switchback occurs. The narcissist will use the victim's

defensive behavior as proof that they are
the one who is the victim. They bring up
past behavior of the victim. The victim will
experience guilt and remorse and will accept this perception.

4. Feels Empowered: Once the victim has
    given up, the narcissist feels good about
    themselves. This justifies their action. But
    every narcissist has a weak point and the
    power they are feeling right now will wane
    until they attack again.

Here's an example of the cycle of abuse in action:

Feels Threatened

Steven recently applied for an upper-level position in his department. He's been at the company
for over fifteen years and has always thought that
he has done a great job, so he is sure that the job
will be his. Then the news comes that the job has
been given to a new hire from one of their com-
petitors who has five years less experience than
he does. Angry and embarrassed at this slight,
Steven returns home to his wife, Clara.

"How was work? Did you get the new position?" Clara asks.

"No." Steven's response is short and tart, and he immediately goes to bed without having dinner. Clara grows worried knowing that he will be in a bad mood for a while and decides to be careful about what she says and does until it blows over.

Abuses Others

Over the next several days, Steven starts to act cruelly to Clara. He starts insulting her over the littlest mistakes, calling her things like "a moron" and "worthless". Then he starts to criticize things like how she makes burgers or cleans the living room even though it's the same way she's always done it. Finally, about three weeks after Steven got passed up for the job at work, Clara is packing for a business trip that weekend when Steven sees her and demands to know what she's doing.

"I'm packing for the conference," Clara says.

"What conference?" Steven snaps.

"The one I told you about a month ago, the one in Nevada."

"You never told me about that!"

"Yes, Steven, I did."

"You're going crazy, Clara. You never told me about this. Wouldn't I have remembered that?"

"But I did tell you," Clara wavers as she starts to second-guess herself. Had she told him?

"You're losing it." Steven shakes his head and leaves the room.

Clara is left straining to remember if she had actually told him. Suddenly, she realizes that she's not even sure about her own memory or grasp on reality anymore. She recognizes this as gaslighting from the many other times he had done it to her before. Infuriated, she decides to confront him about it.

Becomes the Victim

After her trip, Clara and Steven are out at dinner with friends when Clara knocks over some salt. Steven sneers at her and says, "Way to go, Clara Klutz."

Embarrassed that he's using a nickname that she told him had been used to bully her in school, Clara says, "Stop it! Why do you have to do that?"

"I'm just joking. Why do you always have to make me out to be the bad guy?" Steven counters.

"Just don't call me that."

"Why do you always do this? And in front of our friends?"

"Do what?"

"Embarrass me and make me look like a bad guy when I was just joking around. You try to make people feel bad just because you can't take a joke. Doesn't she?" Steven looks to their friends, who nod. "See, they think so, too. You're such a control freak."

Clara starts to feel embarrassed and guilty, especially with their friends backing Steven up, so she apologizes to Steven. Maybe she really is just taking things too personally, and maybe she can be a control freak, she thinks.

Feels Empowered

With Clara resigned, Steven is feeling empowered again until the next position he is passed up for or he gets a bad review. Then, the cycle begins all over again.

Once you understand this cycle, you can escape it.

Myths

To wrap up the first section of the book, we are going to talk about some myths that people believe about narcissism. Pop-culture tends to get everything wrong about narcissism, but pop-culture is exactly what everybody wants to believe. I'm here to prove those people wrong.

1.   You're either narcissistic or not.

When the term narcissist is used, we group the person with the disorder. However, it is best not to refer to the person using a condition we think they have. A person is able to have varying degrees of narcissism, so the term may not encompass them as a whole.

2. Every narcissist is the same.

No, nobody is the same. While they may meet the criteria for diagnosing, they will have varying degrees of symptoms. There are important individual variations that can't be ignored. One very important example is the malignant narcissist I discussed in an earlier chapter. Not all narcissists are malignant narcissists, and it's best to be able to identify one as these sadistic narcissists will make your life even worse than other narcissists. Not even all malignant narcissists are the same.

3. Narcissists aren't able to create close relationships.

People who are narcissistic may seem like they can't get close enough for true intimacy. But, since most narcissists have an underlying weak sense of self, it might mean that they don't want to allow others to get close enough to peek into their psyches. It is true that they never really get close, but this isn't insurmountable.

4. There are more narcissists among people now than ever before.

It has already been said that the 1980s was the decade of narcissism, which brings about the question of why so many people refer to the Millennials as the "generation of narcissists." If they actually are, then so were their parents. This has already proven that this belief is wrong. In fact, there is more evidence to prove the contrary. Young people now are not more narcissistic than past generations. Lee-Rowland and Barry (2015) studied 2700 16-19-year-olds over 14 different tests and found that they had no time-bound changes in narcissistic personality. Media is over-selling this belief that the younger generation believes that they are more entitled. [3]

5. Narcissism is a "thing."

As you have found, narcissism isn't something that you can see in a person or generation. Narcissism varies for each person, and they can have unhealthier and healthier forms. They get discussed as if they were concrete, but until we can fully understand how our brain functions, things like narcissism stay as a way to organize information.

6. Narcissists are literally in love with themselves.

In conversational English, "narcissist" and "narcissism" are often used to refer to someone who is literally in love with his or herself. However, as showing in the previous chapters, the condition is much more complicated than that. They hold high expectations for themselves and delude themselves into thinking that they are truly that perfect; if anything suggests that they aren't—including their ego mirror—their hidden insecurity will start to leak through and then they will lash out. They aren't in love with themselves. They are in love with an idealized version of themselves and are furious at themselves whenever they find out that they aren't that person.

In the next section, we are going to look at some steps you can take to recover from narcissistic abuse we have learned about so far. And if you like what you've learned so far, or you've found benefit, feel free to leave a review on Amazon. I

really appreciate it as your feedback means a lot
to me.

67

Part Two: Recovering from Narcissistic Abuse

Chapter 4: Kick-Starting Your Healing Process

Are there actual ways to heal even hesitantly from the abuse of narcissists? That's a scary question, isn't it?

You've had toxic relationship after toxic relationship and now you are trying to heal yourself. You wonder if you even have a shot at making progress. Why are you different from all the other people who are trying to heal from narcissistic abuse? You are all doing the exact same things. You've joined hundreds of groups on all the social media sites. You say numerous positive affirmations daily. You read book after book about narcissists. You still aren't sure if you will be able to heal.

Healing is going to be different for everybody, and there are three steps that you have to take before any healing will begin. If you don't do these steps, healing will take longer than needed, if it happens at all.

These three steps are listed below to make sure you don't hinder your recovery. You don't have to do them in the order listed, but you do need to do all of them before you can begin to truly heal.

Here are the three steps to heal from narcissistic abuse:

1. Letting Go

When you have accepted the fact that you have to detach from this person, you have to let go. This is similar to accepting but it involves shifting internally. This is the process of deliberately realizing you can make it alone and you don't need that narcissist in your life to emotionally survive.

You think that if you let go of the narcissist, you won't be able to feel good about yourself. You have accepted in your mind that the road will be hard—you might even feel like you have lost a part of yourself—but you have to travel it in order to truly heal and make room for a reciprocal and loving relationship.

You have stopped waiting for closure and apologies from partners who have abused you. You have released the narcissist. You "drop the mic" and go your own way. The next step is acceptance.

2. Acceptance

When should you let go of relationships? When you have stopped growing as a couple, it is time to let go. You are being abused or manipulated, or the climate of the relationship is built on shame, fear, and anxiety. Your relationship creates more pain than happiness.

What is meant by relationships climate? If you can imagine your relationship as being weather, what is its climate? Do you have lots of sunshine and nice breezes with only a few clouds dotting the sky? Do you have constant tsunamis, hurricanes, and thunderstorms?

Having a relationship with a narcissist would be a relationship full of tempestuous, perpetual cyclones.

When you have figured out your partner is emotionally unavailable or abusive and they have no intention of changing, it is time to accept the fact that you have to end the relationship. Stop hanging on vainly and hoping they will turn back into the person you thought they were when you met them.

It is completely normal to want to make things work when you love somebody. Loving a narcissist is as good as being diagnosed with cancer. Being abused by a narcissist has been related to specific kinds of cancer. If you have been diagnosed with cancer, getting away from them is the first step you could take toward your recovery.

Know that the breakup was imminent and reconciliation is not in your vocabulary. When you do, you will be saving yourself from pain and move on the learning how to have no contact.

3. No Contact

This is always the hardest step when recovering from narcissistic abuse. This is the main step that determines whether or not you will completely recover. You can't do the other steps without it.

Not having any contact has to be enforced in order to let healing energies into your space and to protect emotions. If you have contact and don't block the narcissist properly or you try to stay friends, you might accomplish many things but none of them are going to be healthy or helpful to you. Here are some examples of some self-defeating accomplishments:

- Your abandonment wounds will get worse and this sets you up for annihilation.

- Takes away credibility from the boundaries you have set.

- Your confidence and self-esteem will hit an all-time low because you can't accept that a narcissist can't commit even though they pretend they are going to. You will be completely crushed when you realize they lied.

- Come across that you are accepting their wrong behaviors.

- Your feelings of self-loathing will deepen since you keep hoping they will reciprocate your devotion or emotions.

- You will constantly be looking for signs that you can reconcile.

- You become a safety zone when the narcissist needs more than their new victim is willing to give them.

- You are setting yourself up for a "no strings attached" situation. At least it will be from their side.

You have to work through all of these steps to start your recovery. This is why you can't just twitch your nose and make the pain from the narcissist go away. Your relationship is the collection of all your emotional trauma that you haven't resolved, whether it is romantic or not. Some of these might go all the way back to your childhood.

People who realize they have to end the relationship, I mean completely let it go and set in place the no contact, are people who successfully move toward healing.

Chapter 5: The Reality of Healing

"Get over it? How can I get over it? He wooed me, promised my mother she would never have to worry about me. He paid for the wedding. I couldn't even see that he was controlling every part of it, down to my dress and weight. It became clear. I tried, but his control was unbearable. Six years later, we hadn't had kids and I wanted to leave. He lost it. He sent 'proof' to the elders of my church that I was an adulterer. But he was cheating on me. Two years and a lot of money later, I finally was rid of him. How do I learn to trust after all of this?"

This is a common story from people who have suffered at the hands of a narcissist. I understand this difficulty because I have been there. Recovery isn't easy. How do people recover from a loss, especially when it involves a breakup of important relationships? Some of the issues have to do with how it started, who broke up with whom.

In order to break off a relationship, both parties have to be on the same page to end it. The problem is, the narcissist doesn't want out. This means that there will be re-traumatization because the narcissist will try to find a way back into your life.

This is what makes recovering from narcissistic abuse so much more difficult than other abuses. It gets super complicated for those who are married with children to a narcissist. Divorce is possible, but it won't be without a fight. Plus, the emotional recovery will most often than not be put on the back burner, especially if the children are still young. Here's an example:

A woman was married for five years and she has been divorced from him for 12 years. She still considers the divorce ongoing, even after finalization, because he continues to torment her and their children. She had to fight through two custody battles. She, unfortunately, blames herself. She noticed the mistake she made immediately after their wedding. She tried to recover from the abuse and has a therapist, but he won't leave her alone. Until the children are over 18, she won't be able to fully cut him out of her life.

What makes this kind of abuse so difficult to recover from? A narcissist has worked hard to contradict everything you believed about human beings. What you thought you believed about loyalty and truthfulness has been kicked to the curb.

All divorces and breakups are hard, but when it comes to a narcissist, it belies how recovery normally works. It has been proven that people who get out of tough relationships grow, so why isn't it easy for a narcissistic relationship? The truth—you never had a happy moment. Think about the movie *Casablanca* when Ingrid Bergman thinks she will stay with Humphrey Bogart, but he says she must go with her husband. She says, "What about us?" He replies, "We'll always have Paris." While they may be sad their relationship is ending, they will also have a happy moment that they can look back and remember.

In many relationships that end, there will come a moment after all the shouting, screaming, and crying has ended, where you have a moment of detachment and calm when you are ready to move on. With this, you find your "We'll always have Paris" memory when you can remember the good times.

You don't get this when you have been with a narcissist. You don't have Paris. Every moment you spent together, every promise they made, every connection you thought you had gets burned away. You have to recover from war, not from a loss of love.

Just to drive home this point, and to help you understand why recovery is going to be tough, here are some things that make recovery difficult.

1. Nothing is what it seems.

This is the main reason why recovery is tough. Everything that seemed to be about the two people in a relationship turned out to just be about one, the narcissist. Once you have realized this, you will find that you revisit what you thought was happing and what actually was.

2. The fact that hindsight is 20/20.

Those red flags people talk about, the signs intelligent people wouldn't miss but you did, pop up all over the place. Everything that you missed is now in plain view. This is probably one of the most devastating things that I went through. Knowing that I gave my heart and soul to somebody and then was led to a trap is disheartening. Connecting these dots does not help with recovery.

3. You feel foolish.

People who are insecurely attached will often fall into the trap of self-criticism. They blame themselves for all the bad things that happen to them, instead of seeing it as mistakes that anybody could have made. This is an easy trap to fall into in the aftermath of abuse. This will impede your recovery if you can't work through it. Taking re-sponsibility for your mistakes is one thing, but it's another to beat yourself up for making a connection with them.

4. You feel powerless.

A narcissist is only okay if they feel powerful. The only way this can happen is if they make somebody else feel powerless. When you are constantly on the defensive, it's hard to find emotional balance and in control of your life. You may be going through your day doing what you are supposed to be, but you are working on autopilot. This can get in the way of recovery.

Speed Up Healing

With all this in mind, let's look at a few ways to speed up your healing process.

1. Cool Processing

When thinking of the different events, try asking why you felt the way you did, not what you felt. Understanding your feelings improves your emotional intelligence and gives you the ability to label things and manage them in the future. Try to look at things from a distance.

2. Personalize

People end up becoming armored and embittered because they extract lessons from the behavior of a person and then apply it to everybody. Stop yourself if you find yourself saying, "All men are control freaks" or "Women do whatever they can to get what they want." You have to remind yourself that you are talking about one bad seed, not the entire tree.

3. Self-compassion

It's easy to find yourself having a pity party or diving into a poll of self-criticism. Try to develop some self-compassion. Instead of judging yourself, be understanding. View your experiences as part of a large picture. Be mindful of your painful emotions with over-identifying them.

4. Take the Noble Path

If you do have to face this unlucky path, fight the urge to engage. This is especially true if you have children with this person. Trashing them is not only going to give you a momentary rush, but it will also re-engage you. This is the narcissist's goals. Don't give them what they want.

Detaching from Narcissistic Abuse

Before you can start healing, you have to get yourself out of the relationship with the abuser. This is easier said than done, but here are a few tactics.

1. Absolutely no contact.

Get away from them, move out if you live with them, and block them from your life. Block all their numbers, email, social media, all of it. They are going to try to talk to you. If you have children with them, meet with a therapist to work out a parenting plan. This is a legal document that they can't ignore.

2. Just leave.

While using text to break off a relationship isn't typically in good taste, in this case, it might be the safest bet. Tell them you are done and wish them the best. That's it. Block their number. Any other contact might suck you back in. If you left something in their house unless you must have it back, leave it.

If you live with them, arrange with a friend, family member, or someone else that you trust to pack up all of your possessions and leave when your abuser is not home. Make sure that you have at least one other person with you, preferably two, especially if the narcissist has given you any reason to fear for your safety lately.

3. Think of getting rid of common friends.

If you are friends with people who like to tell you that you made a mistake, tell them you don't want to talk about it. If they continue, cut them out of your life as well. To be healthy, you have to get as far away from them as possible. These "friends" haven't seen the parts of the narcissist that you have.

Unfortunately, you might encounter family members who will be this way as well. Treat them just as you would friends who talk to you this way. They might be family, but that doesn't mean you need their toxic influence in your life. If they haven't seen the narcissist's bad side and won't accept that you know something that they don't, then the least they can do is not talk about it.

4. Assume they have moved on.

Narcissists don't need to heal from the breakup. They must locate another life source. Chances are, they will have moved on within a week or so. While this fact might hurt, think of it as a blessing in disguise. At least it means that you will get away once and for all, and they will never bother you again.

5. Let yourself grieve.

You aren't grieving the relationship. Grieve the person you thought you loved. This is a tough pill to swallow, so take some time. Let yourself cry. You might find it helpful to go through an actual physical grieving process, such as writing a letter or eulogy for them that you then bury or destroy. And remember, that person no longer exists—that person probably never existed except in the minds of you and your abuser.

Get Your Life Back

The hardest thing about recovering from narcissistic abuse is changing the dynamic from living in the pain and thinking about the past to gaining momentum that will provide you with a great future. This was the weirdest, not necessarily the hardest, part for me. I was able to do what I wanted without the fear of hearing my father tell me I was wasting my life or what other choice words he decided to use. To be completely honest, though, it took a long time for that fear to completely disappear.

By following the self-care practices I will lay out below, you will start to gain moment in your recovery. You will eventually find that you can survive without out them, and then you are not to blame.

1. Create boundaries

To start the healing, you have to wear a protective shield. Physically removing yourself from them is best. Memories will trigger pain, which slows recovery. Get rid of them on social media, email, phone, and so on. Throw out memorabilia. If you have to be around them, use what is known as "grey rock." This means you mentally and emotionally disengage. The narcissist won't have anything to feed on.

Another boundary you have to learn is how to say no. This will provide you with confidence and self-respect. Become picky about what you say yes to.

If you absolutely must stay in contact with your abuser, boundaries are a must. In addition to emotionally shielding yourself and learning to say no, you will have to set up rules with your abuser about what they can and cannot say and do around you. If they ignore these rules, don't engage. Just get up and walk away.

More than anything, though, it would be best to just establish and maintain no contact with your abuser.

2. Remove the toxicity

You've got to release all the crap you have absorbed from the narcissist so that you can gain clarity. The best thing you can do is externalize. Journal about things, talk to a friend you trust or talk with a coach. Meet with a support group if you need to. Some other things are yoga, deep breathing, and dancing.

This also means you cannot blame yourself for what has happened. That toxicity against yourself, something else you have gotten from the narcissist, is just as bad for you as internalizing everything you're thinking and feeling about your abuser. Remind yourself that none of this is your fault, and nothing that your abuser has told you about yourself and your worth is true. If that does not work, talk with a friend or someone else you trust, maybe even a therapist, to again talk through the toxicity and purge yourself of it.

3. Accept the truth and forgive

You have to accept the fact that the other person is toxic and hurting you. Realize you have been abused. They used your best parts against you. Since you didn't realize what they were doing, they tricked you. Again, it is not your fault.

4. Change your focus

There are going to be times when you will be pulled to the past. This means there are still some things you need to process. Instead of letting the past steal you away, dedicate some time to do this. The rest of the time, try to be mindful and live in the present. Bring your dreams back to life.

This includes thinking about people from the past such as your abuser. Just because you are wondering about what they are doing in the present does not mean that you are not being pulled to the past. In fact, it's worse. You're pulled to a part of the past that is continuing into the present, trying to call you back and trap you in a memory that you have already escaped. Focus on yourself now, not on then and not on them.

5. Listen

Listen to your inner voice because it will guide you safely along. If you aren't certain about a person or situation, ask your inner voice. If you feel relaxed, that's a yes. If you feel like you are on the fence, then maybe you shouldn't.

Start practicing these daily self-help tips and you will soon start feeling better. Once you are ready, get into some of the bigger abuse healing exercises that we are going to go through.

Chapter 6: Creating No Contact

Having no contact isn't a ploy or game to try and get a person to come back to you. This technique has been distorted in blogs and books as ways to manipulate people into coming back into our lives. No contact is just a way to get rid of this abusive person's toxic influences on our lives so we can live healthier, happier lives while creating our true selves and lessening all the people pleasing. No contact is a key that will lock this person out of our spirit, mind, and heart any way possible.

It is understandable that everybody can't get rid of their abusers. Some might have narcissists in their lives to the point that they don't think they can cut every tie with these people. Others may be a co-parent with a narcissist. In these cases, you can incorporate some of the suggestions in this book to fit your needs. If there is a situation where you have to stay in contact with an ex because of children or a legal issue, keep in as extremely low contact as possible.

The Importance of No Contact

Mainly, we establish no contact so toxic people such as malignant narcissists can't use techniques like triangulation or hovering to win us back. When we establish no contact, we remove ourselves from being their supply in a clearly dysfunctional, non-reciprocal relationship.

My sister, who volunteers with a local group that helps people in domestic abuse situations, told me about a man named Pete who left his narcissistic abusive wife but did not establish no contact because they had children together. They loved their mother and she didn't seem to treat them badly, so he didn't want to keep them from her. However, that meant that Pete was still constantly in her presence. She would use any time that they were together to pick up their old dynamics again, putting him down and gaslighting him by getting mad at him for missing arranged visits that they had never actually arranged. My sister said that one of the psychiatrists working with their group thinks that the wife is a malignant narcissist, a narcissist who has no empathy for their victim and might even sadistically enjoy the pain she inflicts. They are divorced now, but since Pete won't establish no contact until the children are both grown, he still suffers from her abusive ways.

Executing It Effectively

Having no contact means that you can't interact with this person in any way, shape, or form. This includes any virtual or in-person contact. This means we have to remove and block all these people from any social media sources because they will try and attempt to provoke and trigger us through social media by posting updates.

We have to also block them from calling or sending us messages through email. Stay away from any temptation to see what is going on in their lives through other people. Get rid of all reminders, gifts, and photos that are in your computer or environment.

Refuse any requests to meet up with these people and don't go any place that they are known to go. If you need to, take legal action. You have the right to protect yourself. Safety always comes first.

It would also be a good idea to cut all contact with any friends of your ex if at all possible along with removing them from all social media. You might have formed a great friendship with some of them during your relationship, but if your ex is a sociopath or narcissist, they are likely to try to smear your name and you might not get any support from the so-called mutual friends.

My sister told me that Pete also had this problem when he didn't create no contact. He still hung out with a lot of his wife's friends and family, including her brother and a couple of her guy friends from high school. Any time Pete saw them after the divorce was filed, they would get on him for leaving his ex because she was heartbroken without him and the children around all the time. Pete tried to explain to them how she had verbally and emotionally abused him in their relationship, but they never believed him, thinking that she was too sweet to do that, especially if their children still wanted to be around her. Then he tried to tell them about the put-downs and gaslighting during arranged visits, but they scoffed at him and even accused him of purposefully not taking the children to the arranged visits that his ex claimed he forgot (that never existed) just to punish her. After a while, they started to avoid him altogether. It was only through another mutual friend that Pete learned that his ex had been accusing him of all sorts of emotional abuse herself, trying to make him out to be the bad guy—the very reason that this other friend stopped hanging out with the ex's brother and any of the others.

Pete was lucky that one in the fan club believed him over her, but other than that one person, everyone in his and his ex's mutual friend group turned on him because of his ex's accusations.

The narcissist's fan club will be convinced by the false self and the illusion of the manipulator. Think about your ex's "friends" as being in a constant state of glorification. These "friends" are the narcissist's sources of praise, resources, and attention. They aren't going to believe your tales of abuse and might even be so used to the way the narcissist treats them, they can't see when they get manipulated, triggered, triangulated, or sucked dry. It would be best to cut all ties with the "friends" completely and find your own support system that doesn't know your abuser.

Continuing the No Contact

If having no contact is a constant struggle for you, there are several ways you can make sure you stick with it. Be sure you have filled your schedule with activities that you like doing that will distract you from memories of them. These might include things like going to a movie, reading favorite books, taking long walks, watching your favorite comedian on YouTube, or spending time with good friends.

Taking care of yourself is necessary during no contact. You have to take care of your mental and physical well-being by engaging regular meditation, doing yoga to relieve stress and strengthen your body, creating a sleep schedule to balance your circadian rhythms, and exercising each day.

If you were to relapse, it is important to remember not to beat yourself up over falling off the wagon and just continue to keep up the no contact. Relapses are inevitable with addictions, but you can recover with time.

Research shows that being mindful will curb our impulses or addictive behaviors by rewiring the regions in the brain that controls our cravings. There are many apps that provide guided meditations to help you relax. You could also try some experimental healing methods like aromatherapy, acupuncture, or Reiki. These can help the progression of the body/mind connection when healing.

What's more important is you need to develop a better relationship with your cravings to get in contact with your ex. You need to practice mindfulness and radical acceptance. Remember that relapsing is just another part of the addiction cycle. Forgive yourself and keep moving forward.

After you have practiced forgiveness and self-compassion, you have to get back on the wagon if you fall off. Track these urges in a journal to curb them so you won't act on them. Be sure that before you put action to any urge, you take one hour to collect your thoughts and regain your composure. It is going to get easier when you realize that breaking the no contract will not give you any rewards, just a painful experience.

Why Remain No Contact

When we end unhealthy relationships, it often leaves us feeling like we can't cope. Although we know that we don't deserve all the mistreatment and abuse, we might get tempted to stray when we let emotions get a hold on us. Trauma bonds will most of the time keep us tied to our abuser along with other factors like low worth, low self-esteem, and codependency. All these might have been ingrained in us from abusive patterns of the relationship or might have made us stay in the relationship longer than we should have.

Having no contact gives you space to revive and heal yourself from all the belittling influences of your friend or partner. It gives you time to detach totally from the toxic people or person while you move forward in life and pursue your goals. It lets you take a look at the relationship productively and honestly from your own thoughts, emotions, perceptions, and intuition, apart from the abuse or gaslighting from your former significant other.

When you can establish no contact, you are staging your victory and learning to explore your strengths, new freedom, and talents with ease.

Take the first steps to success and recovery by challenging yourself to do 30 days of no contact if this is your first time trying it. This is going to provide you a detoxifying period where you will be able to begin healing in a place that is protective and full of self-love and self-care. It will enable your body and mind to repair itself from all the abuse. Then, once you have used all the resources available, you can maintain no contact and get rid of all the toxic influences you used to be tied to.

I remember one of my older sister's friends was in a relationship with an abusive narcissist. With some persuasion from my sister, her friend left the man and initiated no contact as she moved in with my sister. As long as she was living with my sister, she maintained the no contact. However, after about a month and a half, she had found her own apartment and moved out. My sister told me that not long after that, her friend "coincidentally" ran into her ex at the grocery store and started talking with him again. She allowed him to meet up with her again to give her some things that she had left at his place, and the last that my sister knew, her friend was once again sucked into the cycle of abuse.

When I created no contact with my father, my sister reminded me of this friend as her way of telling me that I needed to make sure that it was absolutely no contact and that I maintained it—no if's, and's, or but's about it. She didn't want me to end up like her friend. Still, it was tough because I knew that meant I was likely not to see my mom very often. At first, I thought I could do limited contact, but he was still causing my ill-effects. I knew I had to do it like my older sister. She helped me, and we become more like family than we had ever before, and she told me one thing I could do that would make things a little easier. She told me to let Mom know that I could see her as long as my dad wasn't with her. So, I extended an invitation to my mom to go out for coffee once a week if she was willing to keep it from my dad. If my dad found out, there would be a good chance that he would "bump" into us. Mom said she would try. We have been able to meet up a few times, not every week, but once or so a month. She also made sure to see me and my sister around the holidays. It's not easy, but once you start feeling happy, it is worth it.

Chapter 7: Rewire Your Thinking

Now that you have moved on, it is important that you rewire the way your brain works. Your brain no longer thinks in normal terms. This will take some work, but once you have your brain working for you again, everything else will become easier.

Rebuild and Strengthen

During this phase of healing, your goal is to find greater acceptance about the truth of what has happened. What we will talk about in this chapter is a never-ending process. These are things that you will have to continue to do. It's easy to allow yourself to slip back into the denial, that's why you have to constantly work and be aware of what your mind is doing. All this is doing is making you a stronger person.

Inner Strengths

A great thing to do at this point is to look at your inner strength that was used to survive the abuse. This could be your intuition, which you may have listened to at the exact right time to save yourself.

Take a moment and reflect on the ways that you just knew how to accomplish something without others telling you. What resources did you have within you to set up boundaries and take action in order to survive and get out?

This is going to help you to connect with your inner strength, and it will let you know that anytime you feel something is off, you will know that you can get out of the situation. This will also remind you of your internal strengths that you can tap into to help you get through life.

Responsibility and Control

There will be things on your healing journey that you can control and others that you can't. Knowing the difference is going to save you a lot of trouble. Letting go of things that are outside of your control will require more self-trust that life happens and most things are out of your control while also understanding that you will know how to work through anything.

The more you own your responsibility, the more likely you are to realize that you can control how you respond. Stronger self-control tells you that you leave behind the past. You will also start to notice that the more you can control your reactions to what life and people throw at you, the better you feel.

Emotional Balance and Triggers

You will experience moments of relative calm and then you will be hit with memories that trigger anger, sadness, grief, resentment, nostalgia, and rage. There will be a lot of ups and downs. As you progress, your moments of calm will lengthen. At first, it could just be an hour, then a couple of hours, a half day, an entire day, then maybe a few days before you hit an emotional low. Each time, you will be able to bounce back quicker from the lows.

Triggers aren't all bad. Triggers are things that subconsciously remind you of a traumatic experience so that you can face it and then release it. This can be scary the first few times this happens. This is a good chance to start writing things down. When you experience a trigger, write it down so that you can start to recognize the different patterns.

Anger processing is extremely important. Anger is caused as a result of a personal violation. Anger is a perfectly fine emotion to experience. Anger works as a motivator to fix what has made you upset. The important thing is that you don't keep the anger bottled up inside of you or it will eat you alive. It can lead to headaches, pain, tension, inflammation, and possibly cancer.

You have to release the anger through your authentic self while in private. Using your voice is a powerful way to release anger because it transforms and empowers your strength after the silence you have had to live with. Hitting a boxing bag, mattress, or pillow is a great anger release. Make sure you don't hurt yourself, though.

Once the anger moves on, you will start to feel more vulnerable emotions. Allow yourself to cry if that's what you need to do. You might feel like you are crying for no reason. Trust me, you might not know it, but there is a reason. Letting yourself cry will bring up some things, write them down. Once this process is over, you will feel lighter.

This was an interesting part of the healing for me. I had an older sister who had gone through this already that was there to help me. After removing my father from my life, things appeared to be going good for me even though my sister warned me about the anger. I thought I'd bypass that part, but then it hit out of the blue. Around the time the fear of him popping back up in my life dissipated, the anger hit me. I was so pissed off that I had allowed him so much power in my life with the excuse of "but he's my father." I didn't know how to handle this anger, so I turned to my journal and sister for guidance, and eventually I was able to control it and learn from it. There is no secret weapon to get rid of this anger, you just have to find your way of expressing it without hurting yourself or somebody else.

Inner Child

Your pattern of neglect or abuse has to start somewhere. Most of the time, you were imprinted from a young age to be drawn toward abusive relationships. In fact, your childhood imprinting may not be all that different from the narcissist's.

These abusive relationships feel familiar when you have become used to feeling a certain way.

This is why abusive behavior is subconsciously related to love in your mind. Until you heal these underlying wounds and take a stance against them, your subconscious is going to continue attracting abusive partners.

Here are a few ways to re-parent your inner child:

First, be child-like. This does not mean being childish. Those are two different things. Childish means being obnoxious and irrational, child-like means look at the world with wonder. Laugh at yourself, embrace the innocence and magic with which a child views their world. Don't take yourself seriously. Be kind and nurture yourself. Remove limiting thoughts because children don't think that way. Just let yourself be you without any judgment or self-criticism. Give yourself things you didn't get as a child.

A part of being child-like is also about curiosity, creativity, and play. Do some things that you have never done before, maybe even something that scares you a little. Have you never ridden a rollercoaster before? Do it! Have you always wanted to perform at open mic night (even if you're not particularly funny)? Do it! Get an adult coloring book, play basketball with some friends, go visit a petting zoo. Do anything that will loosen you up and make you feel like a child again. If it happens to be something that your narcissistic abuser used to make fun of or otherwise keep you from doing, all the better.

Next, be around some animals. The healing power that animals have on stressed, anxious, and traumatized individuals is not a secret. Dogs have been trained to help veterans with PTSD, and some hospitals, clinics, and treatment centers bring in—again, trained—dogs and sometimes Shetland ponies to help calm patients and/or lift their spirits. Some universities have taken to bringing in volunteers with friendly, sociable dogs once or twice a semester—in some places, once a month—in order to help ease students' stress levels, especially around finals. Even some senior centers have residents help care for animals because it gives them a reason to get up and complete menial tasks every day.

Pets bring out the child in you. They show you unconditional love. You nurture them and they nurture you. Many pet owners will often view their pets as their children. This is due to the soul of their pet shining through and acting like a child. They are amazing and caring beings with lots of love to share and all they ask for in return is someone to truly love them back. Moreover, they will make a lot better company curled up on the couch at night than your narcissistic ex.

I practice this with my pets. I have two cats, a dog, and two guinea pigs. Some may say I went overboard, but they keep me entertained and happy.

What if you don't have a pet yet? Maybe you haven't found one whose temperament and care requirements fit you, your schedule, and your needs, or maybe you're living somewhere that doesn't allow you to have pets. Does that mean that your inner child can't also benefit from the love of an animal?

No!

Before I acquired my little menagerie, my sister was more than happy to share the love and responsibility of caring for her two beautiful Russian blues with me. I even served as her pet-sitter whenever she went out of town. Those two gorgeous (though sometimes moody) kitties helped get me through a very tough time. I swear one of them even lay down on my hand when I was considering calling my dad's house to talk to my mom and risk my dad answering instead.

If you don't or can't have animals, there are a number of ways to access them for interaction and affection. Spend time with friends and family who have pets, maybe even ask them if you can pet-sit for them like I did for my sister. If you don't know anyone who has pet you can help watch over, you could always volunteer at a local animal shelter. You can nurture your inner child and help some poor animals find loving homes at the same time.

Self-Talk

It's important that you spot your negative thoughts so that you can create a positive mindset. When a negative or fearful thought pops in your head, change it with a positive one. This takes a lot of mindfulness to constantly be aware of your thoughts.

If you grew up in a home with a narcissist, you were programmed with a paradigm of doubt and fear. This can be experienced in your adult relationships as well. To liberate yourself from these things, you have to rewrite the scripts you were taught.

Here's an example:

Once, I promised my employer that I would get a report to her within three days. Unfortunately, I didn't count on it being so much work or on having so much to do outside of work, especially when my recently acquired guinea pig got sick (apparently, they do much better in pairs). I tried and got it done in my free time, but I still felt rushed. I ended up thinking, *This is awful. If I weren't so bad at planning or so incompetent and lazy, I wouldn't have had to rush this.*

This was the kind of thing my dad would say a lot when I was a kid. If I gave him a permission slip Wednesday morning and he left Friday morning when the permission slip was due without signing it, he'd say something like "This is your own fault, you should have reminded me" or "You should've given it to me when you got it on Monday."

After all those years of hearing this, I ended up internalizing this script. In order to undo it, I will have to replace "This is awful. If I weren't so bad at planning or so incompetent and lazy, I wouldn't have had to rush this" with something like "I did my best. Everything will be fine" or "I did my best given the circumstances. That's all that anyone can ask for. If there's a problem with the report, I'm sure that she'll be willing to work with me to fix it."

Nothing is going to shift until you learn how to master this. When you take your first look at your self-talk, you will see there is a lot of negativity. This is because you have received a lot of fearful and doubtful messages as a child and adult. As you continue to work on rewriting this script, by the end of the first month, you will notice a lot less negativity.

Inner Circle

You're healing and you're changing a lot in your life. The next changes are going to come to your inner circle. You still need to trust others, even though I know that's hard to do after going through this. Take a look at the five or six people that you tend to spend more time with. These interactions can be online, on the phone, or in person. Write their names down and the reason why you like to be around them and how they impact your life.

If you start to realize that their impact isn't positive, then you should start pushing them out of your inner circle. The most dangerous thing about being around toxic people is tempting yourself to be pulled into their reality. You have to maintain your own self-awareness and recognize when somebody is trying to convince you to adopt their perspective.

As you inventory your inner circle, ask yourself if they are toxic and draining you or if they are nurturing and supportive. Notice the way you feel when you start to think about them. Take note of how you feel when you are with them and right after they leave. Assign them a specific ring tone and see what emotions it elicits from you. Write down all these feelings and then make the decision as to whether or not they should stay within your inner circle.

You want to surround yourself with more allies during this time.

Speak Your Truth

Telling your story isn't going to heal you completely, but speaking is how you can take the power away from your abuser. Relentlessly facing what has happened will help you to dissolve your cognitive dissonance and break through any denial that might still remain.

Secrets don't serve people, not secrets like these. Sometimes you even keep secrets from yourself. You may find yourself alone in social terms during this time, especially if you have come to realize that the majority of the people in your life are toxic. You may be fortunate enough to have supportive family and friends. This is also where you may choose to seek out more holistic healing modalities to help.

For example, I speak my truth through this book. I discuss bits of what happened to me and how I found help with anybody and everybody who is willing to listen. If you still aren't completely truthful with yourself, start with a journal. You can even start a blog as a sort of online journal that can help other people find your story rather than you having to go to them. Just be prepared to turn off the comments if you don't want to hear from any trolls.

If you don't have family or friends that you can turn to, find a support group. These can be online or in person, there's even a 12-step group called Emotions Anonymous that can help. Websites like Meetup is also a great place to look.

Through all of this, you need to surround yourself with those you trust and to share your story and truth. Don't hide anymore. It is now your time to shine. You can help others to not make the same mistakes that you did.

Celebrate

As you start making progress in your healing, celebrate the successes you reach, even if they are tiny. These celebrations should be things you love to do. They also have the added bonus of making your inner child happy.

Chapter 8: Healing the Brain from Trauma

As discussed earlier, narcissistic abuse has the ability to physically change the makeup of your brain. If this change isn't healed and the brain returned to normal, you won't ever be able to move on with your life. This can lead to suffering from C-PTSD. Let's take a look at a few things you can do to heal your brain.

Meditation

Finding time to meditate can keep you from doing it. You try everything possible to make time, but everyday life gets in the way. You just can't find time to sit down for one hour.

Extended meditation does have its benefits, but you can boost your brain by meditating for only a few minutes a day. Mindfulness meditation specifically can improve a person's mental and physical health. It helps to reduce blood pressure, cortisol levels, and stress levels.

These tips can help you calm your mind in the busiest of times.

How to do it:

1. Focus on breathing: See how your stomach and chest rises and falls as you inhale and exhale.

2. Scan the body: Look for areas of tension.

3. Observe thoughts: Allow your mind to slow down and check in with your thoughts without judging them.

4. Get to know your feelings: Emotions are temporary, and you make the decision on how you want to respond.

5. Closely watch: Choose an object and lock your eyes onto it like a flickering candle or tree branch blowing in the wind.

6. Chant: Fill your mind with your mantra or a favorite saying. Repeat this three times.

7. Touch: Most religions use some sort of bead to keep count of the number of prayers you've said, and it keeps you from falling asleep.

When to Meditate:

1. Utilize your drive: Use stop signs and traf-
    fic signs as a time to breathe.

2. Take breaks during meetings: Keep up to
    date in your mind during office meetings
    just like you check your phone.

3. Intensify workouts: Check in with your
    mind while you are building your body.
    Meditate while swimming or walking on
    the treadmill.

4. Check in with your partner: Go on a date
    with your significant other or friend. Med-
    itate together every morning and night.

5. Bond with your children: Mindfulness ex-
    ercises are great for children. Do some vis-
    ualization, singing, or yoga poses.

6. Line up: Our lives can be full of lines. Next
    time you are waiting in line at the store,
    meditating will help you pass the time.

7. Don't watch commercials: If you don't like watching the commercials, hit the mute and enjoy the silence.

8. Eat mindfully: If you have had a rough day, do you reach for the closest sweets or cocktail? Try to soothe yourself with a bit of meditation.

Meditation is the healing practice I use the most. Making sure I made time for it was the hardest part, but once I started noticing how I felt afterwards, I made time for it.

Cognitive Behavioral Therapy

Here are the most common cognitive behavioral therapy exercises to help with different treatments:

- Cognitive Restructuring

This is an exercise that is designed to help you examine thinking patterns that are unhelpful. It helps you think of new ways of reacting to situations that cause you problems. This involves you keeping a record of your thoughts, which helps you track dysfunctional automatic thoughts and creating alternative responses. This can be done with a therapist or on your own.

- Activity Scheduling

This is an exercise that will help you engage in behaviors that you ordinarily wouldn't do. This intervention makes you find a behavior you normally wouldn't engage in, finding time to schedule the behavior. It is normally used to treat depression and as a way to reintroduce rewarding behaviors into your routine. This should be started under the guidance of a therapist, but the actual act of engaging in the behavior is done on your own.

- Graded Exposure

This exercise is designed to reduce fear and anxiety by doing things that they fear. This is the most effective treatment for most psychological problems. The theory deals with avoiding things we fear that results in increased anxiety and fear. By constantly approaching things you normally stay away from, a lasting reduction in anxiety will take place. This should be done with a therapist at first.

- Successive Approximation

This is an exercise that will help you tackle over-whelming or difficult goals. When you can break large tasks into small steps or by do a task that is similar to your goal but isn't as hard, you can gain a skill mastery that you need to achieve the main goal. This can be done completely on your own.

- Skills Training

This is an exercise that helps remedy skills deficits and works by role-playing, direct instruction, and modeling. The most common subjects are communication training, assertiveness training, and social skills training. This is most often done with a therapist or in a group therapy setting.

- Problem Solving

This exercise helps people take active roles in finding solutions to their problems. Repeated disappointment or chronic mood problems could result when you take a passive role if difficult problems come up. When you learn how to problem solve, you can regain control and make hard situations more bearable. This can be done on your own, with a therapist, or in group therapy.

Dialectical Behavior Therapy

This is a great treatment for personality disorders, anxiety, depression, and PTSD. Most skills you learn in the treatment could apply to everyone. Most of the benefits apply to daily lives. Here are some suggestions on ways you can become present, emotionally regulated, and more engaged with four simple techniques.

You might be a normal individual or in crisis but knowing what comes from receiving DBT could improve your daily functioning. If you aren't a person who has or is in treatment, what can you do? Here are some easy ways to begin using some aspects of DBT:

- Turn off music

Your favorite thing might be listening to music while driving down the road. This is the opposite of what you need to do. Distractions are fun, but it can set you up to miss something important.

What is the harm? Someone might tell you that listening to music while driving could cause more car crashes. It might keep you from being mindful of what is going on around you.

- Name emotions during a conversation

Everybody has experienced being upset but you might not know why. When you don't know why you are upset, there isn't anything you can do about it. This is when DBT comes in. It encourages people to improve their ability to be aware of their behaviors, thoughts, and emotions in a way that empowers them to manage them better. Sounds complicated but it really isn't. Being able to name emotions is a wonderful place to begin and a good place to practice is in daily conversations. You invited a friend over to dinner: "I'm so happy you came to dinner." If your husband comes home late again: "I get irritated when you come home late without calling."

- Active listening

This sounds easy but have you ever found yourself thinking about what you are going to say before the person you are talking to has even finished their sentence? Everybody is guilty of this. At times, it is due to the conversation being heated or we feel anxious. Whichever, it won't end well. You will say something you eventually regret, or you won't get what you want.

You don't have to agree with what they are saying and I'm not saying to change your tune, but if you can learn to really listen, it will improve your odds of reaching the goal you are looking for. When you actively listen to a person, it will increase the likelihood that they are feeling heard and will give you what you want. Always actively listen to who you are talking with even if you don't want to.

- Ask yourself "Is this worth it?"

You've heard the phrase "spinning your wheels". This phrase makes you see gerbils running helplessly on the wheel. They aren't going anywhere, but they run anyways. If you get upset, you might sometimes find yourself just spinning out of control. You might find yourself banging your head being upset about nothing.

In a heated moment, you might not be thinking straight. You are normally obsessing about what you are upset about and making yourself miserable. You can't tolerate stress.

If you find yourself here, you never do anything that will make it better. Most of the time, you will make it worse and the cycle will continue. Being yourself in the moment makes it hard to see the ineffectiveness of your patterns. The easiest way to stop this cycle is when you notice you are very upset about something. Take a minute and ask: "Is this worth it?" "Do I have control of anything?" "Is my reaction making the situation better?"

The DBT message is fairly clear—it's important to take ownership of your life and you have an ability to make changes for yourself.

EMDR Therapy

Eye Movement Desensitization and Reprocessing therapy is a psychotherapy treatment that helps to alleviate the distress caused by traumatic memories. We are going to cover a brief overview of what EMDR is. You should in no way try to do this by yourself. This is a guided therapy that only a trained therapist can do.

This therapy combines various elements to maximize the treatment's effects. This therapy involves paying attention to three time periods: past, present, future. Focus is placed on the past memories that are disturbing. It is given to present situation that is causing you distress and helps you develop skills that are needed for future actions. These are addressed during an eight-phase treatment:

Phase 1: This phase talks about your history. The initial EMDR processing might direct you to childhood events instead of adult stressors. Clients gain insight into their situations and their stressors, and they begin to change. How long they are in treatment depends on how much trauma and at what age the PTSD set in. People who have one single event could be treated in about five hours. Multiple traumas require longer treatment times.

Phase 2: In this phase, the therapist makes sure the client has many different ways of handling distress. They will teach their client ways to do stress reduction the client can use during and between treatments. The goal of EMDR is to give effective and rapid change while the client stays grounded during and between sessions.

Phase 3 – 6: In these phases, a target is identified and processed. The client has to identify three things:

1. A vivid image related to the memory

2. Negative belief about themselves

3. Body sensations and related emotions

The client will also identify positive beliefs. The therapist will help their client rate their positive belief along with the intensity of the negative emotions. The client is told to focus on an image, body sensations, and negative thoughts while engaging in EMDR.

Phase 7: In this phase, the therapist will ask the client to keep a log of any related material that might come up during the week. It reminds the client of activities that help calm themselves they learned during phase two.

Phase 8: The client's next session will start with phase eight. This phase consists of looking back at your progress so far. The EMDR processes all the historical events, current incidents, and future events that might require various responses.

EFT Tapping

EFT, or Emotional Freedom Technique, is a simple acupressure technique that you can use to stop the feelings of narcissistic abuse in moments.

It is a slightly more controversial method for healing than everything else listed here, mostly because it does have significant support from clinical psychology yet and there is still debate as to whether it has any influence beyond the placebo effect. Nevertheless, many of the alternative healing methods upon which this is based are time-tested traditions such as acupressure and energy medicine. It is sometimes used to relieve physical pain but more often to relieve emotional distress such as anxiety and PTSD, and I have had success with it myself while dealing with the anxiety I've developed from my father's narcissistic abuse.

You know you are experiencing an attack or flashback to narcissistic abuse if you have some of these symptoms:

- Chills or flushes

- Pounding or racing heart

- Terror, feeling that something horrible is about to happen

- Chest pains

- Fear of doing something embarrassing or losing control

- Nausea, lightheadedness, dizziness

- Numbness or tingling in hands

- Problems breathing

These attacks will happen randomly, and you will never know when one is about to happen. You can use EFT tapping anywhere and anytime to stop an attack.

Here is how to give yourself a treatment:

1. Use your middle and index fingers, tap gently on each of the spots for three seconds in the order listed to wake up your energy points.

    a. Crown of your head

    b. Eyebrow: the part of the eyebrow closest to the nose

    c. Side of the eye on the outside corner of the eye socket

    d. Under each eye above the cheekbone

    e. Under the nose

    f. Under the lips

    g. Under the clavicle

    h. Four inches below the armpits on your side

2. Use one hand and touch either one or both sides of the body and face. Start by tapping

on the fleshy part on the outside of the hand below the pinky finger while focusing on your problem. You will begin to feel anxiety and fear. Now tap on the spots while you remember your fearful thoughts or experiences.

Healing a memory means you have to eradicate the feelings that come up when you recall that memory. You are going to be able to bring your past to mind without reacting. If you start to feel anxious, your heart begins to race, or your mouth goes dry while you remember, it just means this memory is still raw and hasn't been healed. Use EFT tapping while you remember the attack until it loses its emotional charge. Tell yourself, "It happened. It's over, I survived, I'm fine."

Yoga

Yoga can help you to heal from trauma by helping to regulate your hormones. During your abuse, your amygdala was working overtime and you had a constant stream of cortisol. Your body was constantly fighting to survive. Yoga helps to stop this fight-or-flight response, giving your body a chance to heal.

This is how I start my bedtime routine. I do some yoga, meditate, and then go to bed. It's been this way since I enacted my no contact with my father. It has helped me through so much. I know this is the one thing I can count on to remain the same every single day.

Here are some yoga poses that you can use to help release trauma and further your healing:

1. Bound Angle Pose

To perform, sit on a yoga mat or towel with your legs out in front. Bring your feet in towards your pelvis until the soles of your feet touch. Allow your knees to drop down as far as they can. Hold this for a few seconds and release.

2. Pond Pose

Lay flat on your back on a yoga mat. Bend your knees and bring your heels as close to your hips as you can, keeping your feet about a foot and half apart. Raise your arms up and around your head and let all the muscles in your body to relax. Hold for a few seconds and then let your feet slide back down.

3. Upward-Facing Dog

Lay flat on your stomach with your hands flat under your shoulders. Push up, straightening your arms, and lift your chest, stomach, upper thighs, knees, and shins off the ground. The tops of your feet should be flat on the floor. Make sure that your shoulders are relaxed and not pulled up to your shoulders. Hold for a moment and release.

4. Lion Pose

Get into a kneeling position with your bottom sitting on your legs. Place your hands on the ground in front of your knees. Move your hands forward a bit until you are leaned over your knees with your back straight and neck in line with your spine. Blare your eyes, open your mouth, and let your tongue hand out like a lion. Hold for a few seconds and release.

5. Pyramid Pose

Stand with one foot staggered in front of the other. The back foot should be angled out slightly. Clasp your hands together behind your back and slowly lower forwards. Bring your hands to the ground and either side of your front feet. Your head should be pointed towards the ground. Hold for a bit and slowly raise back up. Repeat on the other side.

6. Arm Swings

Stand with feet hip apart and start to rotate your torso from side-to-side. Allow your arms to go limp and sling around your body. Once you feel relaxed, slow down until your arms stop slinging.

7. Headstand

This is advanced, so don't do it if you aren't comfortable. Get on your knees and place the top of your head on the ground. Wrap your arms around your head. Raise one foot off the floor, tucking the knee into your chest. Slowly peel the other foot up and carefully raise your legs to extend straight up. Hold as long as you comfortably can and slowly lower your legs.

Zumba

Exercise is always good for reducing stress, including that associated with PTSD, but some forms of exercise can help reduce it a little better than others. Zumba is an exercise fitness program much like Jazzercize started by Colombian dancer and choreographer Alberto "Beto" Pérez in the 1990s. It uses for its four basic rhythms salsa, reggaeton, merengue, and cumbia.

Zumba can be beneficial for narcissistic abuse survivors in an opposite manner to yoga. Instead of balance and calm, it will give you an outlet for pent-up energy and a burst of power. Both will help you learn coordination, posture, and control over your body, and neither is correct nor incorrect. Rather, they are two different ways for getting in touch with your body and yourself.

In addition to the obvious cardio benefits and weight/calorie loss from this program, Zumba is great for you emotionally as well. First, all exercise releases endorphins, which are natural mood-lifters. That effect is then combined with the lively beat of the music, releasing more endorphins and lifting your mood even more. Second, Zumba can increase your confidence. The dancing involved in the exercise means that you will be working on your posture and coordination and will most likely be stepping out of your comfort zone. The aforementioned weight/calorie loss will also make you look better, which will make you feel better about and, by extension, have greater confidence in yourself.

The final potential benefit of Zumba is the chance to join a community. If you join a program rather than finding videos online (which is also acceptable), you will find yourself within a group of people all working towards a similar goal: to partake in this unique exercise. You'll get the chance to stick around, chat with new people, and create a community that you can let into your fold if and when you are comfortable enough to tell them your story. Like with any community, it'll just feel good to know that you'll have somewhere and someone to go to if you need help.

There are ten different levels of classes for different ages and amounts of exertion, so supposedly anyone can participate. You can take it in an official class taught by an instructor certified by Zumba Fitness, LLC, or you can just look up "Zumba" on YouTube and find plenty of free videos to dance your way to less stress.

Art Therapy

Art therapy is a form of therapy that involves creative mediums like sculpture, coloring, painting, and drawing. Art can help people process traumatic events in a way that regular therapy doesn't. It gives you an outlet when you can't express something in words.

Art therapists can help you to identify coping strategies and your inner strengths to help you along with your healing. Clients will often be asked to make a mask or drawing of their thoughts and feelings about their abuse and then they will talk about it.

Art therapy is especially helpful when you have lost contact with your body. It gives you a way to externalize your trauma story and will allow you to safely relearn how to connect with yourself. It's important that you find the right art therapist before you start. Regular therapists aren't always trained in this form of therapy, so you may have to look for another therapist if this is a path you want to take.

Support Groups and Group Therapy

Finding a support group or going through group therapy is always a great option for people who have gone through this type of abuse. There is a difference between the two, so you should make sure you pick your best option.

Support groups are a group of people who meet up on a regular basis to provide each other with support. Common types of support groups are AA and Al-Anon, but there are many more. Regular attendance isn't required, and members come and go. There are no therapists when it comes to support groups. They are led by regular people.

Group therapy provides a little more help. It still involves a group of people with similar problems meeting up to help each. In this setting, though, there is true therapy as it is led by a licensed therapist. This is a more structured setting and typically requires regular attendance.

It doesn't really matter which one you choose. Group therapy will likely cost money while support groups tend to be free. Pick what feels right for you.

Sleep

This might seem obvious, but PTSD and other mental disorders can cost you greatly in the sleep area. They can throw off your sleep patterns, keeping you up at night, and even give you nightmares. Sometimes, they make it hard for you to stay awake during the day. At the same time, not getting enough sleep can also make depression, anxiety, stress, and trauma even worse, creating a vicious cycle that will only send you into a downward spiral.

You must make sure you get enough sleep, normally 7-9 hours a night, depending on the individual. Get to bed around the same time every night and set an alarm to get up the same time every morning. If you're having any difficulties

with sleeping, talk to your primary care physi-
cian.

Chapter 9: Reversing the Damage

This chapter will cover how you can reverse the damage by using different healing practices.

Trauma-Informed Acupuncture

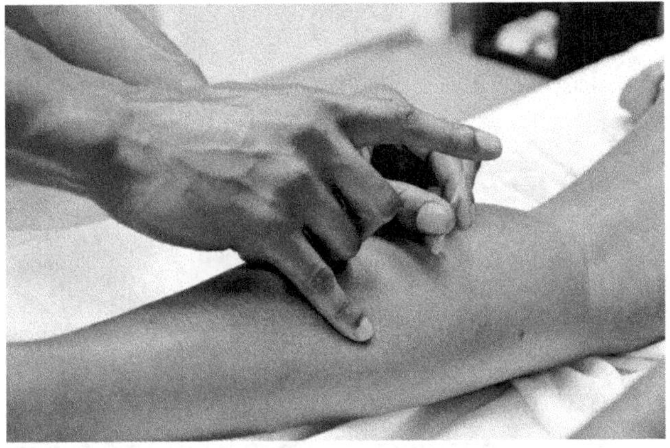

Research has shown that acupuncture is an effective treatment for PTSD. Acupuncture is safe. It reduces chronic pain, symptoms of anxiety, and depression. Acupuncture is a therapeutic option that could help improve PTSD treatments.

Long-term traumatic stress during childhood increases the risk later in life of developing physical health problems, substance abuse, and mental health problems. This study made a scoring system for Adverse Childhood Experiences or ACEs to look at the long-term risk of chronic diseases. It is similar to your cholesterol scores but measures childhood toxic stress. ACEs are associated with chronic pain due to cancer, chronic lung disease, liver disease, cardiovascular disease, neck pain, chronic back pain, headache, and arthritis. People are beginning to seek acupuncture to help treat their pain, most importantly neck and back pain. Some studies say that trauma is more widespread than they once thought. [4]

Community Acupuncture

There are many different delivery methods for acupuncture. It has been the norm in Asia for people to receive acupuncture in a group setting. In the United States, acupuncture for treating substance abuse is done in a group setting. In the past 40 years, the settings have become more similar to a physical exam or massage where just one patient will be in a room or table while the practitioner wears a tidy white coat.

Community Acupuncture is often:

- In a place where many patients receive treatment together

- Accountable and financially sustainable

- Accessible with consistent hours, affordable services, frequent treatments, and lowers barriers to the treatment.

Since acupuncture has been around for over 2,000 years and has been practiced in many different cultures around the world, there are various ways of doing it. There are 361 "classical" acupuncture points along with 48 "extra" points. Along with these, there are many "Microsystems" located in just one part of the body that is used to treat the entirety: the nose, face, ankle, wrists, scalp, hand, and ear. There are also many "lineage" systems that use points that used to be family secrets and were never put on the classical lists. All reports say that each style and system work as well as the next one.

Due to the history of community acupuncture, the core elements of its model line up perfectly with the core elements of trauma-informed acupuncture. Look at it in economic terms, community acupuncture is about high volume and low cost. It wouldn't have been successful if there hadn't been a large number of people willing to try it. Low cost is the main factor that attracts thousands of people to their clinics, but there are other reasons why this model works for people who have a history of trauma.

1. Emotional and physical safety

Acupuncture is a lot safer than most forms of medical care. Serious adverse events are extremely rare. In the United States, practitioners only use disposable needles that decrease the transmitting bloodborne pathogens and infections. Community acupuncture is safer.

Working in a community acupuncture setting but dealing with trauma-informed acupuncture doesn't require the patient to disclose any evidence of trauma. There is just recognition for the need to have emotional and physical safety.

2. Predictability, transparency, and trust-worthiness

The entire clinic is a space of trustworthiness, consistency, straightforwardness, and simplicity. This is needed if the clinic is going to function and be financially successful. These aren't questions about virtue but survival.

Treatments in a community acupuncture setting are very simple. The process will always be the same. A patient comes in for their appointment, check in, find a recliner and get comfortable. The practitioner finds them and asks what they can do for the patient. They have a quick conversation, the practitioner places the needles, and then the patient will relax between 15 minutes to several hours. The practitioner will take the needles out, and the patient will leave the clinic.

3. Support of peers

Most patients have said that being around other people who are receiving acupuncture makes them feel encouraged and supported. Everyone in the room is there taking care of themselves. Sharing healing is one thing that people can lean on without needing to talk about it.

For people who have a history of trauma, relaxing is never a given. Sitting in a quiet room with others who are relaxed can help them take the right steps. It's great to try it since there isn't any interaction required. A person can answer the practitioner's question with just one word: "stress". That is all there is to it. It allows them to turn inward and look at themselves all while being surrounded by other people who are doing exactly the same thing.

4. Mutuality and collaboration

When doing acupuncture in a one-on-one setting, it can emphasize the power struggle between the patient and practitioner. This difference can feel extremely charged for people who have a history of trauma. When a person lies on a table physically, it demonstrates vulnerability and passivity. A person wearing a white coat shows authority and social power. The small room gets dominated by the acupuncturist. This setting shows that the acupuncturist has knowledge about the patient and the patient feels they have to obey the acupuncturist. When the acupuncturist gives the patient advice, the patient feels as if the acupuncturist is trying to control their spirituality, exercise, and what they eat. Medical doctors communicate with a person who has a history of trauma that they are broken. An acupuncturist just fixes them.

Chakra Balancing

When talking about balancing one's chakra, it is only addressing one part of the picture: Every chakra is just one part of a whole system. If you were to look at how chakras work, you will see there is a wonderful connection between each of them and they interact energetically. When you do balance your chakras, you have to consider every chakra and their neighboring centers and the energy throughout the whole system.

There are seven chakras:

- Sahasrara – Located at the crown of the head, it represents the highest spiritual center, the pure consciousness

- Ajna – Located between the eyebrows, it is also known as the third eye chakra and is believed to become more powerful through meditation, yoga and other spiritual practices

- Vishuddha – Located in the throat, it is associated with creativity and self-expression

- Anahata – Located in the heart, it is associated with calmness, balance, and serenity

- Manipura – Located in the navel, it is connected to the power of transformation

- Svadhishthana – Located in the lower reproductive area, it is connected with the unconscious and emotions

- Muladhara – Located at the base of the spine, it is the foundation of a human's energy body

Each of these chakras serves a different purpose; the physical, emotional, and spiritual functions of a human. If one is blocked, it could disrupt the functions associated with that chakra and cause problems with the flow of energy to the rest of the chakras.

How to Balance the Chakras

Balancing the chakras fall into three categories: The ones centered on the physical activity or process, an introspective or meditative practice, and the energy that gets transmitted from you to another person.

Here are some common practices you can do to balance your chakras:

- Alternative or holistic medicine

- Energy healing or hands-on healing

- Breathwork like pranayama

- Meditation, including self-inquiry and chakra meditation

- Exercises that focus on connecting the mind and body, like yoga

There are numerous practices that try to restore the balance in the chakra system to help with wellbeing. The more common ones are:

- Pranic healing

- Craniosacral therapy

- Reiki

Using crystals or stones can also help balance your chakras.

Psychic Cord Cutting

Psychic cords are energy bonds that get created between two or more people. This usually happens when you have shared a deep intimate relationship, but when one partner believes that they are more reliant on the other like being in an emotionally abusive relationship. These cords are created from deeply held patterns and unsatisfied needs. This is why people who have had relationships with a narcissist or lived with one during childhood go through their lives attracting the same types of people.

Psychic cords can cause severe problems on the physical, energetic, spiritual, subconscious, and emotional levels. Psychic cords can cause poor health, weak boundaries, grief, fear, unresolved anger, loss of personal power, repressed self-expression, and blocked creative energy.

Even though symptoms can vary, a person will usually feel drained by a certain relationship when there is a cord present. If we try to let somebody go due to an unhealthy relationship, the continuing energy and cords between them and the other person could hold them back. Below you will find signs that you have developed toxic psychic cords that you need to sever.

Symptoms of psychic cords:

- Can't move on

- Stuck in the past

- Reliving the constant criticism and judgment

- Constant crying

- Thinking about everything they said

- Wanting to seek revenge

- Wanting to go back to them

- Consistently being aware of the bad treatment

- Stalking your ex on social media

- Feeling depressed, angry, and sad about the past

- Constant processing the past

- Insomnia

You absolutely have to cut the cords that are binding you to this toxic person. It not only will sever the psychic ties to the narcissist but will clear away debris you picked up from being around many toxic people. This causes you to attract negative energy.

You can begin by calling on your higher self, spirit guides, Jesus, God, whomever you believe in to help you during this process. See yourself holding a crystal sword. Now say this out loud: "I now cut and release the cords of this relationship with (insert name)." While saying this, move your arms like you are holding the sword and cutting all around your body; remember to cut above your head and say this with intent.

See the sword going below you to cut the relationship's roots. You could also see yourself pulling up the roots and throwing them out of your energy field while constantly cutting with your sword. See the energetic cords dissolving while you cut and throw them from you.

You might realize while doing this that some bundles might be more concentrated near the heart or navel. Intimate relationships are more concentrated in the lower chakras.

You can also do this process to cut the cords with narcissistic parents, whether or not they are alive.

Continue saying their name while cutting the cords. Once you feel like you are done with that person, pause and take a moment to feel whether or not you were successful in cutting the cords. It is best if you only did a few relationships in one ceremony. Begin with ones that stay in your heart or mind the most.

Once you feel like the process is done, pause and take a few deep breaths. See a lavender light circling around you and you standing in your clean energy. Let your heart expand and feel the connection to your higher self. You have created space. When you called on your higher self, you brought to yourself what you need in order to move forward and create new relationships that you have been looking for.

Now, take some time to relax. You may even feel like taking a nap. You might feel peaceful, drained, or hungry. While you are resting, your energy streams disappear as they go back to where they came from.

It is recommended to only do cord cutting once a week. You are going to need time to adjust to the work you have done and give yourself time to create new perspectives.

Essential Oils

To be able to access and then release any emotional trauma, we have to stimulate our amygdala. You can do this through smells. Smell is just one of our five senses that are linked to the brain that houses our emotions. It has been shown to have effects on our limbic system. It also houses anxiety, depression, anger, fear, all negative emotions, and positive emotions.

Essential oils can address symptoms at the cellular level by getting rid of misinformation and re-programming the right information to the cell so that they can function correctly and be in harmony with each other.

Each oil has its own special healing properties. They can be combined for a tailored solution to the health concern you might have. They are even more powerful when used with other healing methods like massage therapy, guided meditation, and energy healing.

Here are the best oils for healing emotional trauma and wounds:

- Lemon Balm

This is the ultimate oil to combat feeling overwhelmed, stressed or for an emotional detox. Lemon balm has been used on the emotional and spiritual realm. It can harmonize the body and mind. It helps people who are highly sensitive and prone to shutting down emotionally.

Use lemon balm to restore clarity and create balance and support the spirit so you might have a more positive outlook on your wellbeing and life.

- Basil

This essential oil can help with feelings of apprehension, panic, or anxiety. It is the oil of renewing yourself spiritually and emotionally. It gives tranquility and strength to the mind and heart. This makes it perfect when you feel fatigued, stressed, or overwhelmed. It might even help you overcome addiction. This helps you overcome self-sabotaging behaviors and brooding thoughts that happen with toxic relationships.

- Hyssop

This is a holy herb that wakes up the heart and brings acceptance while encouraging you to love yourself unconditionally. Hyssop brings clarity to your spirit and encourages emotional well-being and connection.

Hyssop oil is used to get rid of emotional uncleanliness. It can assist to remove fear and guilt from generations of abuse. It purifies for people who believe they have sinned and need to be forgiven. It gets rid of judgment from others and yourself along with limiting old beliefs that don't serve your spiritual path.

- Cedarwood

This oil is great in times of sudden change or crisis like where there is a change in a relationship, job, or household. These events could cause one to feel off balance or isolated. Cedarwood gives you feelings of grounding and stability when things threaten your stability. It can also help lessen fears that keep you from realizing your potential. On a daily basis, diffusing cedarwood could increase your stamina and keep you hopeful, lively, and focused.

- Frankincense

Besides getting rid of depression, frankincense has been called the "oil of truth", since it reveals false truths and deceptiveness. It helps a person to let go of negativity, insults, and lower vibrations. This oil can make new perspectives that are based on enlightenment and integrity.

Frankincense can cleanse the spirit. It helps to remove bad energies that are attached to you. It lets them open up to enlightenment. It addresses spiritual disconnectedness and abandonment.

- Lavender

This essential oil is useful for many conditions. It has been used for stress, panic attacks, irritability, depression, and anxiety. Inhaling lavender oil can enhance the brain's beta waves, and this improves relaxation. On spiritual levels, lavender oil lifts sadness and depression. It brings balance to the soul.

- Bergamot

This oil transfers love back to us. We get so fixated on wanting to make others happy that we forget that we need to take care of ourselves. Bergamot helps us regain self-confidence and relax, has anti-depressant properties, and is uplifting.

This oil helps in areas of self-loathing, self-judgment, self-acceptance, self-worth, and self-love. This oil helps to get rid of fears about not being good enough and holding back because we are afraid of being rejected. It instills validation, and this allows us to accept our authenticity without taking time to worry about other's opinions.

It helps us process and release emotional anguish, toxic shame, need for approval, blame, and fear. It can relieve feeling worthless, inadequate, or incompetent. It helps us to get into our empowerment and confidence.

Spirituality/Faith/Prayer

Included in a person's journey to heal the wounds that lie at the center of themselves is identifying and looking for their self-image that is true and based on spirituality. The main goal is to stay clear of any relationships with the narcissist. This can be done best with a loving and positive replacement.

If you still have a narcissist in your life, you might start trying to be subservient when you are around them, argue with them, and look for approval. These are efforts to achieve what any healthy person wants: not being used or abused, feeling positive and good about themselves, or having an inner sense of value. People around a narcissist might simply be objects for the narcissist to use when they want to. In order for the survivor to get away from the narcissist requires them to be aware of their position, accepting the circumstances, and whatever action is necessary to go forward.

To help one's recovery, establishing supportive and empathic connections are necessary. At the root of a person's inner self is the answer to this question: "Who is in charge of me? Is it the narcissist's demands or opinion of me, my spiritual self, God, my ego, or is it something else? Am I actually able to take back myself?"

The first step when addressing the issue is admitting to yourself how the narcissist has affected you or is currently affecting you. If this is your first time facing this, you might ask yourself if you have some emotional numbness. With all the different levels of abuse, people are going to relate and experience in different ways.

Community is another great thing about find a spiritual or religious path. No matter what your belief system is, there is likely some form of community. This gives you people to be with, connect with, and share with. During my own healing, I finally found my own spiritual belief system other than what my father had forced me into. I found people who welcomed me with open arms and weren't the judgmental people I had grown to know in religious settings that my father frequented. It provided me with a new family.

Here are some exercises that are simple and based on spirituality:

1. Journaling

Find a secure way to express whatever emotion that you have kept inside for a long time. The easiest way is to keep a journal. Take the paper and a pen and write these emotions down. Emotions like longing, grief, fear, sadness, pain, and anger are just some that come up from having been abused. Once you have expressed your emotions, you might have cleared a way to trust in your worth and goodness. This begins when you take a spiritual look through a spiritual lens.

It has been said that humans are spiritual beings. We are different from other forms of life because we have the ability to reason. We aren't just our body, intellect, and mind. You have a power that is greater than you and greater than the narcissist. Knowing this is great when you take into consideration the level of need you have to "worship" them. Take time to reflect on your feelings and begin to cut the cords that we talked about earlier. Think about what you are worth if you based it on spiritual truths and not on the lies and beliefs of the narcissist.

2. Replacing your views about the narcissist

In your journal, choose a page and draw a line down the middle of the page. On one side, write down all the characteristics that your higher power doesn't possess. On the other side, write down all the characteristics that your higher power does possess. Let yourself get completely reflective, open-minded, courageous, bold, and creative about what you would like this ultimate connection to be. Once you have finished, look for patterns. You might notice that you wrote down in the "doesn't possess" list all the qualities that you were hurt by in the past. Maybe you are still being hurt by these qualities either from someone else or yourself. You might have written down in the "does possess" list qualities that you have been touched by through others or yourself.

You might realize that in the list of "doesn't possess" list has most of these qualities. When you go down the second list, a new thought begins to form, and it might be completely different from what you once thought. You might start to feel a sense of hope to start your recovery away from the toxic relationship. You might even start believing that you are a conscientious, empathic, compassionate, and good person. This is the power of connecting with your spiritual or religious side.

Nature

Studies have shown that whether you are in nature, thinking about nature, or looking at nature, it can help you recover from stress, decrease muscle tension, heart rate and blood pressure, lower cortisol levels, and lower activities in the amygdala. If you live close to nature, you can recover from stress faster. Nature acts as a stress relieving mechanism.

Nature can help you heal, get out of the hospital faster, have more energy, have less pain, and feel less anxious. This can be achieved by having a plant in your room, touching an animal, or looking at a beautiful view.

Being exposed to nature can improve cognition, mood, memory, energy, and attention. People who take frequent walks in nature will have better cognition after their walk. For children who have been diagnosed with ADHD, having play areas in nature help them have milder symptoms of attention deficit.

If you would like to be able to connect with nature at any time:

- Take walks in nature

- Keep pictures of nature near you

- Listen to sounds of nature during meditation

- Keep plants indoors that you can tend to

- Exercise outdoors

- Keep a garden or flower bed outside

- Practice mindfulness outdoors

Music Therapy

Music therapy is a great intervention to help traumatized adults and children. In can reduce anxiety, facilitates social interactions, and offers emotional relief.

Musicians have been asked to support the recovery of communities and people after natural dis-
asters and other horrific events. Music therapy
addresses trauma by giving the following:

- Changes like relaxed muscle tension, reduced heart rate, and lower blood pressure.

- Non-verbal outlets for emotions that are associated with traumatic experiences

- Improved feeling of empowerment, confidence, and control

- Reduces stress and anxiety

- Positive and active participant involvement during treatment

- Positive changes in emotions and moods

For individuals who have gone through trauma of some sort, music is an outlet to express emotions. Music therapy lets people know it is fine to feel what you feel. It is fine to acknowledge what happened.

Self-Hypnosis

This is a great way to reduce stress and open your mind to new thoughts and ideas, especially if you are dealing with behaviors like certain addictions.

While using self-hypnosis, you need to think about what messages you would like to give to yourself. Think about some short statements that you want to use when you reach hypnosis.

These statements should be:

- Simple

- Positive

- Honest and genuine

Some examples include:

- To reduce nervousness: "I am a great speaker."

- To help with addiction: "I don't like alcohol."

- To relieve stress: "Work relaxes me."

These statements are messages for your subconscious. Use "I" to focus on certain actions and prepare statements in present-tense. To begin with, concentrate on a few statements. Memorize them and keep them in your mind.

Steps for Self-Hypnosis

1. To begin, you need to feel completely comfortable and relaxed.

2. Find something you can keep your attention and focus on.

3. Focus on the object and clear all thoughts out of your mind.

4. Be aware of your eyes, think about your eyelids getting heavy and closing slowly.

5. Tell yourself that you relax with each and every breath.

6. Visualize a gentle movement of an object going up and down.

7. Slowly, softly, and monotonously count backward from ten to one and say "I am relaxing" after every number.

8. Tell yourself that once you have finished counting, you will be in a hypnotic state.

9. Once you have reached the hypnotic state, it's time to focus on the statements you memorized.

10. Clear your mind and relax before coming out of your hypnosis.

11. Slowly but energetically count to ten.

12. Once you get to ten, you will be awake and feel revived.

Creative Writing

Poetry, short stories, novels, they've all been used to express people's emotions and work through the trauma they've experienced in their earlier lives. Sometimes the trauma is disguised fairly well, but other times, the veil is fairly thin. No matter how or what the final product turns out to be, creative writing can be an excellent healing tool far beyond the initial journaling. Not only do you express yourself, but you get a physical product out of it. Rather that product will see the light of day or not is entirely up to you.

Chapter 10: Creating Healthier Relationships

After I established no contact with my dad, I had a very hard time trusting people. I especially had a hard time with men and other members of my family, my older sister being the only exception. Even as I started to surround myself with people who wanted to help me, like the other people going to my new church, I kept up a stone wall. I stayed focused on healing myself without realizing that I was missing a key part of my healing process: opening my heart.

One day, I was talking with my pastor, and she told me that she could tell that something had been bothering me. So, I confessed to her that I had been enjoying going to the church and meeting with all the different people. I told her that I loved how they were of so many different backgrounds and yet they still opened their arms wide to each other. Still, I didn't trust them. I didn't give her any details, but I told her that I had a not-so-ideal home situation growing up and had only just started to heal from it.

I didn't even have to tell her that I was afraid of getting hurt again. She knew. Instead, she put her hand on my shoulder, looked me in the eye and said, "Naila, have you ever heard a lone wolf howl at night?"

I was confused. "Yes."

"How does it sound?"

I thought on it for a moment before I said, "Sad, maybe even hurt."

She smiled and said, "Lone wolves are ones who lose their packs. They're very sad and can even get injured or sick on their own. But you know what's so cool about lone wolves? They can always find another pack and be made one of theirs. Then they heal and aren't lonely anymore."

That had a big effect on me. From that day on, I did everything I could to open my heart back up to other people. It wasn't easy at first as I was still very timid, but it got easier with time, and soon enough, I felt like a happy lone wolf in her new pack.

After you have rescued yourself and started to heal, you are going to meet less manipulative and abusive characters. You might run into them every now and then since the world is full of them, but you won't let them in to saturate your life like you used to.

How people constantly treat you will get better while you are continually treating yourself better. If people don't meet you with all the respect that you know you are worth, you will immediately see it and get away from them. It isn't going to hurt that much when you have to walk away since you are going to do it faster before any damage can be done. You are going to be more confident about your decisions, too. You aren't going to suffer from the nostalgia that you felt in the past after you left an abusive situation or person. It will be easier to move on after you have been disappointed.

Romantic Relationships

Romantic relationships aren't easy for anyone. Everyone has their own heartbreak story, and those can sometimes end badly enough for people to consider giving up on romance altogether.

When you've been abused or traumatized in any way, this struggle can feel insurmountable. The fear of being lured into a new relationship only to end up stuck on that cycle of narcissistic abuse once again can be too much to bear. That fear is natural. That fear will keep you on alert and help you notice the signs of abuse before it's too late. But you also shouldn't let it keep you from moving on with your life.

It might be hard at first, as with new friendships post-narcissistic abuse. You might even carry trauma related specifically to narcissism in a romantic relationship. Perhaps you're struggling with not generalizing the trauma into hatred of the opposite sex (or same sex, if you swing that way). Maybe your previous partner used to belittle your appearance, making you nervous to undress, or coerced you into doing things you didn't want to do, which has given you an aversion to sex. It could take a while for you to become comfortable with your potential partner, so you will need someone patient. Regardless, once you reach a point where you are comfortable with each other, your partner will become one of the most important supporters of your healing process.

No one should ever build their identity around a romantic partner. However, a romantic partner will help you heal on a more intimate level than other loved ones. They will be your friend and confidante, someone who will help remind you that what the narcissist said about and did to you was never true and never about you. You must still be the facilitator of your healing, but your partner will be cheering you from the sidelines.

Now, something I hear all the time is that abuse survivors are afraid of entering into romantic relationships that are just like the narcissistic relationship they left. They worry that they only attract those kinds of people. Honestly, even though my narcissist was my father, I worried about the same thing. They say that daughters marry their fathers, after all.

But you know what? You now have all the tools you will need to escape a toxic relationship in time.

If you begin dating somebody new and you realize they are attempting to disrespect or manipulate you, you are going to have the self-trust, clarity, and strength to end it. Walk away with your integrity and dignity intact. You can leave situations and relationships with gratitude rather than resenting it as you did in the past.

Remember, everything will be fine just so long as you don't stop working on your healing because you are in this new relationship. If your new partner asks about what you are doing, be honest but only tell them as much as you are comfortable with telling them. Just say you are not ready to talk about the rest yet if you don't want to tell them everything. If they respect your choices and support you in whatever way you need them, then the two of you are on the right path.

Relationships with Other Survivors

Admittedly, these will take a little more work than relationships with people who have not been through abuse like you have. On the one hand, you will have someone who won't just empathize with your situation—they will understand it firsthand. On the other hand, it will be hard to avoid each other's triggers and make sure that you are each as comfortable as possible. Still, you will probably make quite a few friendships—and possibly something more than a friendship— through such things as support groups and online chats for survivors.

My sister and I both suffered from our dad's narcissistic abuse, and it was my sister who convinced me to go no contact with my dad in the first place. We didn't have to worry about being judged for our emotional scars because we had been through similar situations. We could talk freely about what happened when we felt up to it, and when we didn't want to, we helped each other forget about it. My sister even introduced me to other survivors, and my support system continued to grow.

These aren't relationships that you should turn away just because you have both survived toxic relationships. Instead, you need to support each other. If they want to talk about it, just listen. If they don't want to talk about it, don't. They'll talk about their experiences when they're ready, just as you will talk about yours when you're ready, so just be content to be building your new pack.

Chapter 11: Creating a New Life Post-Narcissism

This is when you need to integrate and incorporate all the insights and lessons from your journey. This is when you learn how to reintegrate socially into the world. During this stage, you will continue to use the techniques from above to continue with your life and healing process.

Choices

By this time, you have realized that you have many more options than you thought were possible. You can now begin to make choices more easily since you have gained clarity, confidence, and strength.

Up to this point, you have noticed the way you feel and how you validated these feelings. Those feelings were very unpleasant during the time you were processing through all your past while opening, purging, and finding new possibilities. During this time, it is important to focus on the way your heart likes to feel. Try to work and place yourself in that state wherever you may be and whatever might be happening around you. You don't have to keep your feelings hostage to the people and events in your life.

If you begin feeling bad, you can now regulate your feelings better with talking to yourself like, "I don't have to feel like this. The way I feel is my choice. How would I like to feel?"

People are always saying, "Let it go and leave it there," but this can make you feel invalidated and it isn't appropriate to where you are in your journey. It is completely impossible to let it go and leave it alone since there is a lot of questioning, restructuring, processing, revisiting, and understanding to do. By the time you get through all the processing, the "let it go and leave it there" is the choice that takes you to learn how to thrive.

Owning Reality

By now you feel more assertive and you own your reality. If other people try to gaslight you and make you doubt how you perceive reality, you won't fall for it and you won't gaslight yourself anymore, either.

You completely trust yourself now. You can stand confident and strong against negativity and oppression when other people try to confuse you. You also know when things happen that you need to work on and you just keep pushing through.

Plan for the Future

You can truly see, dream, and plan for the future you want to have, and you can continue to move in that direction.

You are more focused on building a future instead of living in the past. The past won't come up as often and if it does, it won't cause the emotional turmoil it did earlier. You will soon see that old emotions almost don't exist anymore. It is a lot easier and faster to get through things and get yourself out of unpleasant emotional times without being weighed down by the past.

When you are dusting out corners and tying loose ends, you are preparing for the things you are creating. You will have purges throughout the process to get rid of old emotional energy that is still holding on to your body so you can go forward without it.

You spend more time looking toward your future and doing things to help you get there rather than staying in the past. You are interested in your future rather than the past. What is most important is that you believe in your ability to make the future what you want it.

Relationship with Fear

Face your fears as they happen. You might want to create your own catchphrase such as "no, thank you" or "get out of my face" to keep your fears in place. Adding in some humor might help when they come to the surface. They are going to back off faster now because you feel safer.

The fears will begin to pass just like empty thoughts that don't trigger an emotional response. This lets you become an observer. This is your highest awareness that recognizes how quickly you get fearful and begin to panic. If you try not to engage with it, it will be useless unless it becomes a matter of life or death and the fear is needed to get you to safety.

More Resilience

During this time, people are going to test you. Good news is that you aren't going to react the way you used to. This isn't saying you aren't going to feel hurt when people hurt you, but you won't fall into their trap of reacting emotionally to their crap. You will be able to see it for what it is, instead of giving them power and losing self-control.

When you don't give your power to others who try to rattle you by evoking a negative emotion, you won't let what they said or did eat at you after. Things might surprise you, but you will realize what is taking place and you will be able to redirect your emotional power to the way you would like to feel, rather than the way others want you to feel to meet their demands.

It will be easier to shift into a positive state if something were to knock you down. Earlier when something knocked you down, you would fall, and it would be difficult to get back up. You won't go into a downward spiral. Now, it is closer to just tripping on a crack in the sidewalk that you didn't see, you catch yourself, and keep walking.

Keep using controlled challenges to master your traumatic experiences. These challenges make you expose yourself to the things that scare you so you can reclaim activities and places that used to overpower you. You will quickly see how fast you can go back to places you once went with your ex, watch the next season of your favorite television series, or face whatever in your past that might cause pangs of loss and nostalgia as well as other emotions.

You remember that pain has an evolutionary purpose. It is meant to tell us that something we are doing or interacting with is not good for us and we must adjust our lives in order to avoid that negative influence. How you react to the negative influence causing the pain is all up to you. You can either let it get to you, or you can learn from your past experiences and not give the negative influence power over you.

Purpose

You will be focusing on getter better clarity all around you, your sense of purpose, and then live that purpose. Your purpose is to express your soul to the world. It becomes your WHY. Your purpose is the things that matter most to you. It isn't a goal or destination but instead something you live each moment of each day.

If you would like to make a change in your life that will last, you have to know what your sense of purpose is. By now, you should be feeling more driven. Even if others try to use your energy to respond to their "emergencies" and put their fires out, you will be able to stand clear and firm with your boundaries around your energy and time. Using your sense of purpose as a filter, you can set boundaries you need so you can keep contributing good to the world, focus your energy, and living your truth. You used to feel guilty when you prioritized your work or yourself, but you know that is the best thing to do for yourself and the people around you.

You might have occasional pangs of guilt that might rear their ugly head, but you can remind yourself to focus on what is true and let it go. Sacrificing your sense of purpose and energy to meet other people's demands isn't on your plate anymore.

Speak Your Truth to Community and Family

You might decide to speak your truth to a family who is supportive of you or you might decide to confront your abusers. It all depends on the situation. You might even want to talk with your community or organization. It isn't necessary to confront your abusers, but it might be helpful to speak with your abuser in the community or family and have others witness it. It gives them an opportunity to admit what they have done and then to make it right. Remember to listen to your gut feeling when deciding whether or not to confront them.

If you do decide to speak your truth or confront people about their abuse, remember not to expect anything to change within the other person or the relationship. You can't control any of that. This is about empowering yourself to speak up and face your fears about speaking the truth to your oppressors. If you give an opportunity to your abuser and they refuse to admit they're wrong or they only give you excuses, you will know the abuse will continue if you continue to have contact with them since they justify their behavior rather than accepting responsibility.

Never expect an apology or validation. They aren't going to own up to their wrongdoing because if they are a narcissist, they don't have a sense of responsibility. Remember that your community and family might or might not believe you, and that isn't relevant to your truth. These people aren't good for your wellbeing or sanity if they don't believe you.

Remember you have to stand strong without worrying about how others are going to react. Don't subscribe to their reality especially if they try to minimize it, shame you, blame you, guilt trip, or try to pretend it didn't happen. Keep telling yourself that it isn't your reality. Now you have to walk away.

Forgiveness

During this time, you will be working to learn how to forgive yourself and others. This isn't saying you are going to reconcile all those relationships or stay in contact with your abusers. It doesn't

mean that you have to forget everything that happened.

Having no contact or very little contact is what you are looking to do. This will help to protect your wellbeing, sanity, and peace. Forgiveness is about having contact or letting them into your life. It is about getting rid of harsh feelings, such as resentment, bitterness, and anger, that keep holding you back from experiencing abundance and joy in life.

When you remain resentful and angry, you will continue to attract others who remind you just how resentful and angry you are because they make you feel resentful and angry. Having harsh feelings brings bad karma to you. It was a very dirty trick that your abuser played on you by transferring their negativity to you by their be-havior. You, of course, are resentful, bitter, and angry because they did awful things to you. It is important that you see all this. Now is the time to work on releasing any of these harsh feelings that remains so you can return the karma to the owner and replace the harsh feelings with peace.

Some people are unfavorable toward forgiveness and that is perfectly fine. You might hear others talk about having a fear of going back to their abuser if they were to forgive them. This is understandable. At times it might be safer to not forgive so that you can remember why you have stayed away from this person, especially if the relationship is full of guilt such as a family member. If the abuse has gone on for many years, it is possible that you might not feel like forgiving because there was a lot of harm done to you for a long time.

You may eventually get to a point in your life where you will be able to forgive your abusers if you met them in your adult years since the duration and depth of abuse haven't been so long. You might not be able to forgive a parent since it was a lot of abuse for a very long time and it just won't ever be made right. This is very true if they refuse to admit what they did or change their ways. If you were married for 20 plus years and they did you a lot of harm and you just don't want to forgive them, that is perfectly fine. Just continue to work on releasing the harsh feelings that are left that keep holding you back and ruining days.

Keep in mind that you are doing all this for you not them. The biggest challenge is will you be able to get to a point where you don't get consumed and you don't think about them as often. If it does come to mind, you have a clear head to know that you have been hurt beyond any restitution and it is your right whether or not you want to forgive your abuser.

Once the fight is done and you have peace of mind, this is what I like to call forgiveness. You aren't internalizing the shame you felt from being abused since you know that it isn't your burden. You have to be very clear with yourself that the ones who abused you don't have a place in your life because they aren't willing to change.

Forgiveness is a gift that you bestow on yourself. Forgiveness happens in layers, just like healing. It isn't like going from one day to the next. Completely forgiving yourself is going to take time. It is amazing when you reach a moment when you are ready to let negative feelings go that you have toward one of your abusers. Those feelings miraculously fall away and leave a space for liberation, peace, and openness for new possibilities for the future and present. You don't need to try to forget what happened since the memories are what remind you that contact with your abusers might be dangerous. When you see the same patterns happening with others, you know you can't let it happen.

Forgiving yourself is the hardest since we constantly blame ourselves and regret your actions and this only puts you in a negative loop. You can empower yourself by seeing the things that you have learned for the experiences and you won't react the same way if something were to happen again. Think about how you would do things differently the next time and how you can keep your integrity. This helps you forgive yourself when you can't protect yourself and you lose your integrity in these moments. The self-hatred and self-hate will eventually go away, and this is when you know you have truly forgiven yourself.

Self-reliance

You have been learning how to have more self-reliance and you are validating your truth more than you worry about what other people think. You have realized that you have wasted a lot of energy worrying about what other people think.

Your barometer that wants approval is facing inward rather than outward. Whatever might happen now, you are able to trust your own instincts to be able to fix it. You know you have the awareness, tools, and strengths to go with whatever life might throw at you. You will be able to make decisions that you need to in order to thrive and take care of yourself.

Reconnection

To quote Judith Herman, "Recovery is based on the empowerment of the survivor and the creation of new connections. Recovery can take place only within the context of relationships; it cannot occur in isolation."

You are building a group of wonderful, loving, and supportive people in your innermost circle. These are the people who you truly, deeply value their relationships. There is a lot of trust between the people of your inner circle and you. You are creating a new family, even if your tribe isn't related by blood. They don't play games, they don't manipulate, and they won't use you for selfish reasons. They will have your back and want what is best for you. They genuinely care for you. They won't say things that will tear you down or make you feel small so that they will be able to feel better about themselves. They will celebrate your success and will encourage you. They won't depend on you to fix or rescue them. They understand they need to do that for themselves.

If you are thriving, your relationship will have a "win-win" quality and they will feel uplifting instead of draining. You will be able to reintegrate yourself socially within the community. When you meet people or are hanging out with your people, you won't talk about your past. You are focused on the future and present that you are making right at the moment. Since the past isn't consuming you, you can connect with other people who haven't been abused by a narcissistic person.

You can form healthy balances of social and alone time. This balance depends on whether you are more introverted or extroverted. Introverted people will recharge their batteries alone. You have a small group of very close friends and you like to hang out either one on one or in very small groups. Extroverted people recharge their energy around others and know a lot of people. They enjoy spending time socially instead of alone.

You will be more focused on creating a spiritual connection with the universe and yourself. That devastating feeling of loneliness that has followed you your entire life isn't with you anymore. You might see a glimpse of it every now and then, but it won't last and you know how to get yourself out of it fast.

You are finding deep in your soul, body, and mind that you will never be alone since every single thing that lives will dance, breathe, and sing together and you are a part of everything. You feel peaceful and calm when you are alone and in situations where you are surrounded by others that you don't feel a connection with. At the deepest level, you can feel your connection with the universe and yourself along with other people who are close to you and this lets you thrive.

Self-trust

You aren't confused about whether situations or people are right for you. You know and trust your inner knowing. It could take you a moment or two to realize it in some instances, but you will get it and then take actions to support and protect your peace.

You no longer second-guess your intuition and aren't willing to sacrifice your peace. When someone is trying to manipulate you and tell you that you are wrong and you need to believe them, your new level of self-trust lets you make decisions with clarity and ease.

You don't allow yourself to believe what you want since you are willing to see what is in front of you and you take action rather than fantasizing about a potential outcome.

Get Out of Drama

You don't have any energy left over to be involved in other people's drama and games. It is easy to direct your resources and energy toward your purpose and passions to what feels right and good for you since it will give you a sense of meaning.

At this stage, you don't care about people who feel angry or jealous that they aren't getting everything they want from you or the people who like to spread rumors about you since you decided you weren't going to put up with their abuse.

You aren't seeking approval from anyone, so it is easy to steer clear of their games. You have accepted the fact that there is going to be people who hate you and that's fine since this means you are doing things right for you. You might even laugh at those attempts. You realize how silly they are, and you won't fall for them. You have a great sense of purpose and self-trust and it is stronger than any hurtful comment that anyone makes.

You don't feel the impulse to lower yourself just to make others comfortable. You also don't waste your energy trying to defend yourself from the false provocations and accusations. You spend your energy on your purpose and building your dreams while trying to make a difference around you.

Closure

You might actually not ever get closure from a narcissistic abuser since they won't let that happen. There are things you could do to help stop the cycle.

Getting closure from your abusive experiences begins when you can own your truth even if the organization, community, or abuser doesn't believe you, doesn't show remorse, or refuses to own responsibility for their actions. When you begin speaking your truth to other survivors of abuse and professionals who understood what happened, you feel more confident to speak up and tell your truth or share it in videos, blogs, and books.

Never underestimate how powerful speaking your truth can be. You will see just how brave you are when you can speak your truth. It can transform your life and will give others the confidence to tell their stories.

Keep your focus on gratitude in order to open a path to abundance. You need to find something grateful for your experience to focus on. You don't' have to be grateful for the person but the experience. Figure out what you found out about yourself and your life and see how it transformed your life. Reflect on the lessons you've learned that you can take forward.

When you are able to create meaning from your experience, you will change the trauma into a new purpose. This is where you find the gold.

One Last Reminder Before Conclusion

Have you grabbed your free resource?

A lot of information has been covered in this book. As previously shared, I've created a simple mind map that you can use *right away* to easily understand, quickly recall and readily use what you've learned in this book.

If you've not grabbed it...

Click Here To Get Your Free Resource

Alternatively, here's the link:

https://viebooks.club/freeresourcemind-mapfornarcissisticabuserecoveryintox-icrelationship

Conclusion

Thank you for making it through to the end of this book. Let's hope it was informative and able to provide you with all the tools you need to heal from the wounds of narcissistic abuse.

Recovery from any problem is never easy. Recovering from abuse is no different than recovering from an addiction, but both are worthwhile and will improve your life. You have to take things day by day, believe in yourself, and put yourself first. Abuse is an unfortunate norm for the world. Many people don't even notice, while others pretend it doesn't happen. But if you can stand up and end your lineage of abuse, you can inspire another person to do so. Don't continue to live with it because you think you have to. You don't. Nobody has to. Seek help and change the world.

Sincerely,

Naila Farrah

P.S.

If you've found this book helpful in any way, a review on Amazon is greatly appreciated.

This means a lot to me, and I'll be extremely grateful.

Helpful Resources

You shouldn't have to go through this battle alone. Here are some resources should you need them in your journey separating from your narcissistic abuser:

Substance Abuse and Mental Health Services Administration: https://findtreatment.samhsa.gov/

Help for male survivors: https://malesurvivor.org/

US National Domestic Violence Hotline: +1-800-799-7233

Yes I Can: http://yesican.org/

Suicide Hotline: 1-800-273-8255

Notes

[1] Shanta R. Dube, MPH, MD, MS Robert F. Anda and MD Vincent J. Felitti. "Childhood abuse, household dysfunction, and the risk of attempted suicide throughout the life span." *JAMA* (2001): 3089-3096

[2] Stinson, FS, et al. "Prevalence, correlates, disability, and comorbidity of DSM-IV narcissistic personality disorder: results from the wave 2 national epidemiologic survey on alcohol and related conditions." *J Clin Psychiatry* (2008): 1033-1045

[3] Dingfelder, S. "Narcissism and the DSM." *Monitor on Psychology* (2011): 67

[4] Lee-Rowland, LM, et al. "How do different dimensions of adolescent narcissism impact the relation between callous-unemotional traits and self-reported aggression?" *Aggressive Behaviour* (2017): 14-25

Related Books That Might Benefit You

Co-Dependency: The Crazy Codependent in Toxic Relationship - The Codependency Cure, Healing & Recovery from Trauma for Emotionally Healthy Love Relationships with Partner, Parent, Mother or Father

This POWERFUL Guide Will Help You Overcome & Recover From Codependent Relationship & Cultivate Your Own Growth!

Do you often feel guilty when you're not able to help someone who completely depends on you?

Are you feeling like you don't have the freedom to explore opportunities for growth?

Do you feel like you can't live up to your full potential because you have to take care of everyone's needs before your own?

If you want to stop all these in your life, then keep reading...

A codependent relationship can feel like a burden on the person bearing the brunt of other people's problems. Being in it often leave you feeling used, unappreciated and angry. Most times, you feel almost forced to help certain people solve their problems as you feel compelled to pacify their negative emotions, give various suggestions, or offer unwanted advice.

Margot Fayre, Doctor of Psychology, knows this all too well. Once in a codependent relationship herself, she knows how frustrating and limiting all of this can feel like. This was the impetus that drove her to write her book, so she can help people like you overcome codependency using science-backed insights.

Are you ready to find out if you're being taken advantage of, end your codependent relationship, and finally set yourself free?

Co-Dependency, the only book you'll ever need to finally overcome and recover from a codependent partner, friend or relative who hampers your growth, and start cultivating emotionally healthy relationships.

Here's a taste of what you'll discover inside _Co-Dependency_:

- **_Definitely understand what it means to be in a codependent relationship_** so you can make the necessary life changes using SIMPLE techniques

- **_Quickly discover what your triggers are_** so you know how your mind works and EASILY put an end to your codependence issues

- ***Firmly set your personal boundaries*** and COURAGEOUSLY assert yourself so you no longer need to depend on anybody

- ***Effectively make changes within*** using mindfulness and practical methods based on PROVEN psychology principles

- ***Take absolute, full responsibility for your own emotions*** and resolve conflicts using FIELD-TESTED methods

- ***Fast-track your journey in recovering from co-dependency*** by figuring out and tapping into your GREATEST strengths

- ***Become a better partner, friend and family member*** by becoming a GREAT team player and advocate

And much, much more...

If you're ready to finally take back control of your life, live up to your maximum potential, and say

goodbye to your controlling relationships, now is
the time.

Emotional Abuse Recovery: Men & Women Suffering in Silence - Emotionally Abusive, Destructive Relationship or Marriage with Manipulative, Toxic People (Healthy Healing and Recovering from Trauma)

<u>Stop Suffering In Silence & Finally Heal From Emotionally Abusive Relationship With The Help Of This POWERFUL Guide!</u>

Are you constantly feeling emotionally tortured and betrayed by someone you used to love and adore?

Do you see no point in even trying to get out because your abusive partner has taken full control of your life?

Do you feel suffocated and helpless because it just seems like no one understands, or knows how to help you?

If you want to stop all these in your life, then keep reading...

Going through, and subsequently healing from emotional abuse is easier said than done. Most times, abuse victims feel blamed for staying or getting themselves into that kind of relationship in the first place.

Abuse survivor turned domestic violence advocate, Marjorie Lise, knows this story all too well. Lise had stayed with her abusive partner for an entire decade, before realizing that she deserved better. In her book, she talks about how she was able to successfully stop suffering in silence and finally escape her abuser, with the hope that her experience will inspire others to take back control of their lives, too.

Lise wants people like you to know that there is HOPE!

Emotional Abuse Recovery**, the only book you'll ever need to get out of an emotionally abusive relationship and finally start to heal!**

Here's a taste of what you'll discover inside *Emotional Abuse Recovery*:

- ***Unmistakable signs to watch out for*** to accurately recognize and effectively address toxic relationships, manipulative people and emotional abusers

- ***Destructive ways that emotional manipulation*** can affect a person for the rest of their life

- ***Detailed and clear guidelines in taking the first steps*** in dealing with your abuser, starting the healing process, and taking back control of your life

- ***Proven methods in creating an airtight safety plan*** that will help you get out of EVERY sticky, abusive situation

- ***Effective techniques to maximize the positive effects*** that guided journaling can do in easing negative emotions stemming from abuse

- ***Actionable tips that help you be and stay strong during the critical recovery stage***, so you won't feel the need to give in or go back to your abuser ever again

- ***Highly reliable, helpful, and easily accessible resources*** that you can use whenever you need emotional, physical, and mental help

And much, much more...

If you're ready to finally heal from your trauma, experience emotionally healthy relationships that you deserve, and say goodbye to your abusive torturer for good, now is the time.

Did My Narcissistic Mother Love Me?: Dealing with Manipulation & Trauma from Narcissist - Healing & Recovery of Narcissism Abuse in Toxic, Abusive Family Relationship with Parents, Mother or Father

Discover The PROVEN, Most Effective Ways To Heal From Abusive, Narcissistic Mothers & FINALLY Thrive In Life & Relationships!

Are you feeling overwhelming resentment and anger towards your narcissistic mother and some of your family members?

Do you struggle with regulating your emotions and letting other people in?

Do you feel frustrated because you can't seem to find a way to heal from your emotional wounds and establish healthy, loving relationships with others?

If you want to stop all these in your life, then keep reading...

One of the most difficult things for wounded children to accept is the fact that there is a very small chance that their narcissistic mothers will ever change. At best, they will look for ways to address their toxic traits and grow for the better. However, narcissists _rarely change_... and if they do start acting nicer, more often than not, it's because they seek to manipulate.

Award-winning author and narcissistic abuse survivor, Nanette Abigail, knows a thing or two about this sensitive issue. Her own

experience with getting out of a controlling relationship with her mother equipped her with the
insider knowledge, that had allowed her to finally
wake up to the reality that the problem wasn't
her, and that what she went through wasn't her
fault.

In her book, Abigail lays out the crucial tools
she used to set boundaries, create safe havens,
and find mental clarity for herself... and with her
help, you can, too!

***Did My Narcissistic Mother Love Me?*, the
only book you'll ever need to heal and
move forward with life after suffering
emotional turmoil from narcissistic parents.**

Here's a taste of what you'll discover inside *Did My Narcissistic Mother Love Me?*:

- ***7 Essential facts adult daughters***
  with a narcissistic family need to be aware
  of, so they can FINALLY see and accept the
  hard truth

- ***Expert-approved methods to identify that VITAL moment*** your Psychological Immune System starts kicking in and field-tested ways to effectively boost it

- ***Eye-opening insights to understand WHY*** you grieve for the loving mother you never had, so you can finally start to overcome your negative emotions and destructive attachment

- ***Important first steps to kick off the process of healing*** from the toxic, narcissistic relationship you have with your abusive mother

- ***Proven ways to deal with your anger***, so you can clearly understand the reality of the situation you were in as you start your narcissistic abuse recovery

- ***Foolproof techniques to skillfully detach from and set healthy boundaries*** with a mother consumed with narcissism

- ***Practical tips in maximizing healing benefits*** of mindfulness as you recover from your abusive parents

And much, much more...

If you're ready to finally learn how to deal with, set healthy boundaries, heal from your narcissistic mother, and say goodbye to the overwhelming feelings of helplessness, now is the time.

www.ingramcontent.com/pod-product-compliance
Lightning Source LLC
Chambersburg PA
CBHW061753250726
48657CB00001B/106